Literacy Leadership

for Grades 5-12

Rosemarye Taylor
Valerie Doyle Collins

Association for Supervision and Curriculum Development ❖ Alexandria, Virginia USA

Association for Supervision and Curriculum Development
1703 N. Beauregard St. • Alexandria, VA 22311-1714 USA
Telephone: 800-933-2723 or 703-578-9600 • Fax: 703-575-5400
Web site: http://www.ascd.org • E-mail: member@ascd.org

All Web links in this book are correct as of the publication date below but may have become inactive or otherwise modified since that time. If you notice a deactivated or changed link, please e-mail books@ascd.org with the words "Link Update" in the subject line. In your message, please specify the Web link, the book title, and the page number on which the link appears.

Printed in the United States of America.

s2/2003

ASCD product no.: 103022
ASCD member price: $18.95   nonmember price: $23.95

Library of Congress Cataloging-in-Publication Data
Taylor, Rosemarye, 1950–
    Literacy leadership for grades 5–12 / Rosemarye Taylor and Valerie Doyle Collins.
       p. cm.
Includes bibliographical references and index.
    ISBN 0-87120-745-1 (alk. paper)
   1. Language arts (Middle school)—United States. 2. Language arts (Secondary)—United States. 3. School administrators—United States.
I. Collins, Valerie Doyle, 1955– II. Title.
LB1631 .T245 2003
428'.0071'2—dc21

                                    2002153096

12 11 10 09 08 07 06 05 04 03   12 11 10 9 8 7 6 5 4 3 2

Literacy Leadership
for Grades 5–12

Acknowledgments

In reflecting on more than 30 years as a teacher and administrator, I am amazed at how consistently the challenge of improving literacy and serving all students equally has been placed in my path. There must have always been a plan that I didn't see. In response, I've done my best to find research-based ways to help all students become joyful, independent readers and writers. I am especially grateful to all those who have challenged, supported, and taught me how to be a better leader and educator, especially Bob Williams, Jay Taylor, and Ted Hasselbring.

—Rosemarye (Rose) Taylor

It took eight years as a part-time student and a full-time mother for Annie McGhee Owens to complete her college degree and begin teaching. Her persistence, dedication, and passion for learning placed an indelible mark on my life. I have patterned my own career on her example, understanding that all students are capable of so much more when we believe in them and provide the teaching and direction they need. I will always be blessed and thankful for her, my mom. I am also grateful to my grandmother— my cheerleader—who just missed this book's publication, and to Shannon, Seth, and Chandler Collins, the men in my life.

—Valerie Doyle Collins

1

Committing to Literacy Leadership

Ramon sits quietly in his seat. He lets his mind wander as the teacher stands in front of the class talking about yesterday's homework assignment. He likes where he sits in the first row, fifth seat, because the teacher almost never looks in his direction and he can just blend into the class. He notices his classmates begin to clear off their desks and sees that they are taking out their World Cultures textbooks. Ramon begins to worry that the next assignment is to read from that dreaded book. His worst fears are confirmed when his teacher tells the class to open their books to Chapter 6 for group reading. He has heard this before and he knows the routine. Each student will read one paragraph out loud as they go in order through the class. Maybe today she will begin on the other side of the class. No such luck as she tells the first student in his row to begin. With a lump in his throat and beads of sweat forming on his brow, he quickly scans down to the fifth paragraph, hoping that it will not be too long or too hard. His heart sinks when he sees the first word of the paragraph, *Mesopotamia.* As he looks over the paragraph, he also encounters *Egyptian* and *pyramid.* A sense of panic surges through him as he tries to figure out a way of avoiding reading out loud in class. He thinks about pretending he is sick or asleep. Finally he decides to go for a sure thing, so he reaches over and punches the boy next to him on the arm. The boy screams and Ramon is relieved to know that he will not have to read in class today. (Blase-witz & Taylor, 1999, p. 33)

RAMON'S STORY IS NOT UNIQUE. IN STUDYING OLDER, STRUGGLING READERS WE found that they repeat over and over again the coping mechanisms they have developed to either avoid reading and writing or to hide their lack of literacy skills. Most often they act out, disrupting the class in some way, and become "discipline problems." By the time these students reach 5th or 6th grade, they know they don't read as well as their peers and believe that is just how it is. They believe that no matter how hard they try, they will never become readers and writers. Their self-defeating beliefs lead to poor school-related self-esteem. All these factors contribute to great academic frustration, and, when coupled with early adolescents' developmental needs for peer approval and independence, a downhill slide may escalate into a crisis.

The political scrutiny and criticism regarding the lack of an acceptable level of literacy among diverse student populations has made educators well aware of the need to improve literacy learning. In the past, we assumed that students learned to read in elementary school; if they did not, we found alternatives for them in middle school and high school—alternatives that rarely led to academic success or to graduation. By middle and high school (the thinking once went), students should no longer be learning to read, but reading to learn . . . reading to master higher-level content, concepts, and skills. Today we acknowledge that many students, perhaps as many as 50 percent, leave elementary school without developing the reading skills necessary to succeed in middle and high school. We recognize that this skill deficiency severely affects not only their performance on standardized assessments, but also their success in all content classes. For this reason, we believe that supporting literacy is every educator's job—at every level and all day long.

This book focuses on the end goal for literacy learning: *that all students will become joyful, independent readers and writers.* It does so by exploring fail-safe literacy leadership, which provides administrators (school-based and district) and teacher-leaders with a deliberate and purposeful process to maximize students' literacy achievement and help them to become not just better readers and writers, but also better listeners, speakers, and thinkers. We've chosen the term *fail-safe* because the essential components of the system we suggest, when implemented as we suggest, will ensure your success in improving student results. In our experience, texts and consultants focus on one component or another, but do not combine leadership processes with strategies for adolescent literacy acquisition and development. That combination is key. Blending leadership processes with knowledge of adolescent literacy development will allow all faculty members within your school to work together to strategically develop a plan to achieve your literacy goals.

To reach these end goals, it's up to leadership—school administrators, primarily—to get the ball rolling. The first task in developing a fail-safe system of literacy for your school involves three steps:

1. Believe that all students can be joyful, independent readers and writers . . . and that you can help them reach that goal.
2. Evaluate your fellow stakeholders' commitment to all students becoming joyful, independent readers and writers.
3. Demonstrate your commitment through action.

Let's get started.

Step 1: Believe that all students can be joyful, independent readers and writers . . . and that you can help them reach that goal

As busy administrators, most of us don't take the time to think about what we really believe, select what is most important for our professional lives, and then focus on that one issue no matter what else arises. The first step in improving the literacy of all students in a middle or high school is to believe that through your leadership, you can significantly influence students' day-to-day learning and help bring about measurable improvement in their reading, writing, listening, speaking, and thinking skills. This initial step is critical because it will serve as a continual reminder of the end goal and help you develop strength for the task of leading and inspiring others.

> **Valerie:** *Whenever I reflect on how powerful our individual beliefs are, I think of an old story about an observer on a construction site. The observer went over to a bricklayer and asked, "What are you working on?" "Laying brick," grumbled the first man. "It's back-breaking work, but at least it's a paycheck." Then the observer went over to a second bricklayer and asked the same question. The response was a little different: "I'm one of the construction workers and we're building the east wall of this structure." When the observer asked the same question of a third bricklayer, the response was*

quite revealing: "I'm helping to build a cathedral, and one day right here where I'm standing the spirits will rise high above us, and people will be meeting to worship and be educated!" While all three bricklayers had basically the same job assignment, their vision and commitment varied greatly. The third man felt his work had a powerful purpose and connected his personal mission to that of the larger work.

Right now you may be wondering how this story relates to your work of literacy leadership. Think about the various people you interact with in your school regarding the subject of students' literacy learning. No doubt, some are like the first bricklayer—teachers who just check off the assessed skills when they are designing a lesson, doing the work because it's their job to do it. Others believe their job is to prepare students for standardized assessment, and that literacy skills are a necessary means to that end. But those who will make the greatest difference are the ones who might say, "I'm helping young people develop into good readers and writers so they can be productive, happy adults!" Fail-safe literacy programs are founded on educators' conviction that the goal of literacy is attainable. And to believe that, we must believe in both our students and ourselves. By beginning with an examination of your beliefs about your literacy work and then seeing how your beliefs align with the common vision of the school, the students, the teachers, the community, and the district, you can go on to fulfill your leadership role with astounding personal and professional satisfaction and effectiveness.

Step 2: Evaluate your fellow stakeholders' commitment to all students becoming joyful, independent readers and writers

Once you have examined your own beliefs and have committed to all students being joyful, independent readers and writers, the next step is to reflect on the commitment of the environment in which you find yourself. Just as your belief system and commitment influence your decisions and behavior, the belief systems and level of commitment among your staff, students, and other stakeholders influence their decisions and behavior . . . and ultimately, affect the success of your literacy mission.

A few years ago, the two of us learned a valuable lesson about environmental commitment to and belief in all students. With our personal commitment as district and school-based administrators, we set out to provide support and opportunity for our most needy middle schools (two schools where students' mean reading comprehension scores were 13 and 18 on the Stanford 9). We had district financial support to provide smaller class sizes, new technology, and new learning tools for teachers and students. We were committed to ongoing professional development for the principals and teachers. Everything was set. Or was it?

It turned out that the environment was not a receptive one. When we met with the faculties to offer new learning tools, professional development, and literacy-related opportunities for students, we were surprised at the less-than-warm reception we received. Both sets of teachers clearly communicated that we, the district and school-based administrators, did not understand their schools or their community. It didn't matter that one of us (Rose) had actually attended the first school as a student and the other (Valerie, the newly appointed principal) had attended the second. We heard comments such as, "You don't understand our students," "They are doing their best," and "We know how to teach them; they need strict discipline or they get out of control!" Although we were disappointed in the teachers' responses, we hoped they would adjust and learn a little more about how to support the students, even though the effort would require them to make some changes. Those who did not want to focus on literacy learning were supported in locating another position in another school.

Likewise, when we met with the parents and a district representative from the community to share the need for modifications within the two schools and the opportunities that would be available to the students, we were surprised to encounter their disbelief in the need for change. The parents voiced unwavering support for their schools as they were and for the teachers. They said things like, "Our teachers are great!" "Our children are learning a lot," and "Our students don't need technology and new materials."

Although we presented both the parents and the faculties with the achievement data and current research on the possibilities we could provide for the students, neither group accepted that the students were not achieving, or that they needed a different learning experience. We were unsuccessful in this literacy leadership experience because we failed to accurately evaluate the stakeholders' belief systems and their commitment to helping every student fulfill his or her potential and become a joyful, independent reader and writer.

You'll want to avoid pitfalls by asking yourself these environment-focused questions: Are the demands placed on you by the system or district reasonable and will they support your commitment? Do the teachers believe that all students can become joyful readers and writers? What about the school leadership team's commitment to all students? Does the school community believe that all students can become joyful, independent readers and writers? What about the community beyond the school? Most importantly, do the students know that there is a belief and an expectation that they will all become joyful, independent readers and writers?

Valerie: *As a principal, I found myself wondering how to begin working toward achieving the vision I had for all students to become joyful, independent readers and writers. Our middle school's mean percentile in reading on standardized assessment was in the lowest quadrant and seemed to be accepted by everyone! The district, in its commitment to the students, community, and teachers, had designated the school as one to focus on literacy learning. The expectation was clear that this approach would improve students' reading, writing, and math achievement.*

I quickly found that my unwavering commitment to literacy was paramount. How else could I mobilize the students, teachers, community, and political forces to collaborate in working to meet the district expectations? Many people were looking for a weakness in my leadership so they wouldn't have to follow through on the expectations we had set for ourselves and the students. In addition to my own commitment, I needed the commitment of all the stakeholders to effectively bring about change for the students. I needed to realistically evaluate the commitment of the stakeholders so that I could strategize to develop a collaborative team. I also recognized that to effectively influence the stakeholders' sense of efficacy, I needed a good idea of where they stood.

To begin this process yourself, focused on your own school and stakeholders, review the examples in Figure 1.1 and the subsections that follow

EXAMPLE

FIGURE 1.1
Stakeholders' Commitment to Literacy Learning

Stakeholder	Perceived Level of Commitment (please circle)			Comments
Students	Low	Medium	(High)	They try to meet expectations of teachers.
Teachers	(Low)	Medium	High	They believe that students do their best and that there's little point in asking for more. Regard content teaching as their job, literacy as somebody else's.
School Community	Low	(Medium)	High	Supportive, but each year more parents seem to be exercising their school choice option.
School Leadership Team	Low	(Medium)	High	Overworked! Team members don't want another responsibility.
District or System Leadership	Low	(Medium)	High	They want us to focus on accountability for test scores—and do it quickly!

to stimulate your thinking about key environmental considerations. Then fill out the template provided on page 10 to capture your perceptions of your stakeholders' level of commitment.

Students. By and large, students believe that their achievement is directly related to their ability. Most accept their achievement (whether low or high) as "fixed" and do not see that a change in the effort they invest or in the practices their teachers use could make a difference. These students lack a sense of efficacy—a belief in their own ability to alter the academic direction of their lives. Most students don't see how the test scores affect them anyway. Ask yourself: Do your students understand that regardless of their current reading level, they can improve their reading, writing, and testing skills? Do they know that printed texts carry messages and can bring them joy? Do they have choices in what they read and see meaning in what they read?

Teachers. Often, dedicated staff have spent years working in lower-performing schools or teaching lower-performing students and may lose their vision of excellence for the reluctant reader. They may need to see what "average" and "above average" looks and sounds like to have measure for comparison. Do your teachers understand the different needs of the older struggling reader? Do they have the knowledge and skills to incorporate the processes of literacy, literacy strategies, and independent reading into their instructional plans?

School community. Older reluctant readers may find themselves in communities that acknowledge the need for literacy, but don't know what to do with them as older students. In many cases, the volunteer literacy tutors who enjoy working with young children are less comfortable working with middle or high schoolers. It doesn't help that many of the natural challenges adolescents face, including curiosity regarding new ideas and the "adult" world of sex, violence, and drugs—can be exaggerated in lower-performing, frustrated students. Ask yourself: Does your school community understand the needs of older struggling readers? Their desire to be seen as independent and self-sufficient? Their reluctance to ask for help? Their great concern about peer approval and sensitivity to being "different"?

School leadership team. The entire school leadership team, consisting of the principal, assistant administrators, and teacher-leaders, must share the commitment to all students being joyful, independent readers and writers. Will your colleagues on the team support this commitment in their daily decisions? Will they consistently communicate this commitment to all stakeholders? Will they work to limit classroom distractions? Are they willing to model the love of literacy for teachers and students?

System or district leadership. Today, virtually all school districts voice the need for higher test scores and change, but at the same time, they may encourage administrators not to excite their community, teachers, or students in the process of pursuing these goals. Communities, teachers, and students tend to be loyal to their schools and believe that although there may be some negative press, their personal experiences are generally good. Extreme change in a school can create discomfort for the teachers, which is quickly transmitted to students and parents. Influential parents tend to resist the idea of change; they want their children's school to be like school was when they themselves were students, even though today's students and the demands we place on them are much different. Even if a school needs to change, the last thing the political powers want is for teachers, parents or students to complain that things are changing and that the changes are creating discontent.

Research on the phenomenon of change reports that although it usually takes three to five years for measurable change to emerge, just initiating the process may create anxiety for those who will be affected. Ask yourself: Will the political establishment in your area support the change—and support *you* when and if teachers or parents resist? As a successful associate superintendent in an urban district was fond of saying, "The trick to success is to look like you are innovative, while you are really status quo." This cynical statement reflects a rather common perception of just how much change political structures tolerate. How much change will your political structure tolerate? Will your elected officials support more professional development for teachers, along with new instructional strategies, learning tools, and classroom environments?

Before moving on to the next section, fill out the template in Figure 1.2. You'll find it a useful resource as you start strategizing for success.

TEMPLATE

FIGURE 1.2
Stakeholders' Commitment to Literacy Learning

Stakeholder	Perceived Level of Commitment (please circle)			Comments
Students	Low	Medium	High	
Teachers	Low	Medium	High	
School Community	Low	Medium	High	
School Leadership Team	Low	Medium	High	
District or System Leadership	Low	Medium	High	

Step 3: Demonstrate your commitment through action

You have now examined your belief system and made a commitment to all students, and you have examined the commitment of stakeholders within and outside of the school who affect your planning for a fail-safe system of literacy leadership. Finally, you are in a realistic position to demonstrate your commitment through action.

Other than writing about your commitment to literacy in official documents like school improvement plans, how will you show the students, teachers, school community, district, and system what is most important to you? No, you can't just run through the halls shouting out your priorities all the time, but you can make them clear through the decisions you make. Perhaps you think that you are so busy working to create a positive learning environment for students and teachers that you can't think about doing anything else. On the contrary: Focusing on your priority—that all students will become joyful, independent readers and writers—will make your job easier because you can use this priority to guide other decisions related to the commitment of school resources and your own conduct.

First, how you make, communicate, and carry out decisions about the allocation of school resources—financial, human, and material—will model for everyone what you believe to be important and serve as the foundation for how others perceive you as a literacy leader. Think about your commitments (the current status of things and your pledge to make changes where needed) in each of following categories, and then fill out the template provided on page 14.

Financial/budget. The most obvious category of resource-related decision making is how you, as principal, allocate your school's financial resources. Do you fund literacy after everything else is in place, or do you budget for literacy first and everything else second? Do you consider literacy to be equal to all other budget considerations, or is it more or less important? If there isn't enough money to go around, what steps have you taken to seek *additional* literacy-focused funds from the district, state, or community agencies? Are you willing to reduce funding or delay funding for another need in order to fund literacy?

Personnel. The next big demonstration of your literacy priority (linked closely with the budget) is how you allocate and use personnel. Does your school have adequate staff? Are the class sizes small enough so that reluctant readers can receive the support they need? Are you using personnel in a way that will maximize students' opportunities to become joyful, independent readers and writers? It requires courage and commitment to make personnel decisions differently than they have been made in prior years. Are you up to the challenge?

Professional development. If you have budgeted and allocated personnel to demonstrate commitment to literacy, do these teachers know how to teach reading and writing to adolescents? Do they incorporate literacy strategies into their instruction or do they just assign reading and writing? Recently, a school administrator confided in us that her school has grade-level reading specialists, but these individuals are not trained in adolescent literacy and aren't particularly effective at improving student achievement or helping classroom teachers to do so. Providing reading, language arts, English, and content area teachers with ongoing, literacy-focused professional development is a visible and important way to act on your commitment. In Chapter 5, we discuss how to design a professional development plan for literacy success.

Learning tools. Once you have collaborated with your staff to create clear expectations of a classroom for literacy learning, you will want to provide the best available learning tools to the students and teachers. Classrooms across all content areas that use literacy to improve student achievement must incorporate learning tools in addition to the course textbook. This is another budget-related issue, but it is a philosophical one as well. You may find that the real cost of a budget item is not so great once the research has taken place and the learning tools selected are aligned with your priorities and the needs of the students. Creating a classroom for literacy learning, as well as locating and selecting the best available learning tools for your students, is the focus of Chapter 4.

Learning space. If, when translating your priorities into actions, you find that you need smaller classes, you'll also need more teachers, who will require more space. Providing the space and infrastructure necessary to support literacy sends a strong message to your students and staff. You might wonder why we are addressing space, but for many schools, finding adequate teaching space is a real challenge. Space also translates into budget concerns.

Learning time. Research proves that time is a variable administrators can manipulate to improve student performance. Is literacy afforded equal time in all content areas? For students who are not good readers and writers (those who score below the 40th percentile on assessments), is becoming a stronger reader and writer *as important* as developing skills in the various content areas? Is it more important? Creative scheduling allows school leaders to make it clear what the priorities are. We need to maximize the use of learning time and eliminate time wasters and interruptions. Even with these efforts, some students will require more time than their peers to become joyful, independent readers and writers. Where will you find the time? During the school day? Before or after school? On weekends? Perhaps even outside of the traditional school year? When it comes to clarifying for the school and community what is important to you as a school leader, your decisions about how time is used to support literacy may be among the most important decisions you make.

After you've reflected on your commitments in each of these categories, record them in the template in Figure 1.3.

As important as it is for principals to demonstrate their commitment to literacy through the way they allocate school resources, the school community will also perceive their leadership in terms of what they say and how they spend their professional time. Think about it: When there is an important athletic event, is there any question that you want the school's team to win? You probably wear your school colors and pins to make it clear that your school's team is important. More than that, you probably attend these athletic events, greeting parents and students and cheering the team on. It's plain to all that you care and that you are interested in your athletes' success, sportsmanship, and behavior.

The same tenets go for literacy. If you spend your time in classrooms, asking students to see their writing, asking about what they are reading, and celebrating success, you are sending the message that reading and writing are important. Perhaps you can share your favorite book with students, or let them know if you write or publish. Sometimes we think that

TEMPLATE

FIGURE 1.3
Resource Commitment to Literacy

Resources	Commitment Level	
	Current Status	**Level Pledged**
Financial/budget		
Personnel		
Professional Development		
Learning Tools		
Learning Space		
Learning Time		

everyone knows what is important, but be careful not to make that assumption. Be explicit and think about how you demonstrate your literacy leadership through allocation of resources, your time, your actions, and what you say.

We find a great example of a commitment to literacy leadership in action in Dr. Francis Catalon, principal of Crispus Attucks Middle School, located in one of the poorest communities in Houston, Texas. During the past two years, Francis has made his priorities and commitment to all students becoming joyful, independent readers and writers clear to everyone in the school community. Students, parents, and teachers have observed their principal's communications, resource allocations, use of time, and actions to be consistent with these high expectations. He has committed to long-term professional development for the entire school, new learning tools for the teachers, and modifications in the school schedule. He has made changes in personnel to improve learning for students. Those who visit Attucks Middle School today see a positive change in the learning environment and in the literacy strategies used in the classroom. Soon they will see changes in student achievement. Under the literacy leadership of Dr. Francis Catalon, the transformation has begun.

In the Classroom

When Dr. Paul Van Mitchell was appointed principal of Colonial High School, with its diverse student population of 3,400, it was ranked seventh out of 12 high schools in its large, urban district. Student achievement was low, but many accepted it because of the school's high poverty rate and the fact that 75 percent of the students attending spoke English as a second language.

The new principal had different beliefs. Van believed that the students could perform better and that he could affect that performance through his work with the school community. He spent most of his first month on the job in classrooms listening to students, taking note of what they wanted and what they needed. He did the same with teachers and community members. What Van learned was that they all wanted to have a school that was respected and that they could be proud of. With all of the stakeholders on the same page and making a commitment to improve achievement, Colonial High School's hard work and upward spiral began.

After five years, the school is now ranked fifth out of 14 high schools and competes favorably with those that have many more advantages. How did Van achieve this improvement? He would say that he didn't—that he has just served the students, faculty, and community. His service has been through relocation of resources, learning space, learning tools, and time; through professional development; and through curriculum realignment.

If you ask the school community how their principal shows his commitment to literacy learning, they will say he shows it by being in the classrooms. He has a goal of being in 25 classrooms each day—quite a feat for any high school principal. While in classrooms, he continues listening to students, working with them, challenging them, and sometimes teaching them. He reflects with teachers on what is working and how they can serve students better. Dr. Paul Van Mitchell is a fail-safe literacy leader whose actions have lead to measurable improvements in literacy learning.

Review and reflection

As we outline here, getting started on developing a fail-safe system of literacy for your school takes just three steps:

1. Believe that all students can be joyful, independent readers and writers . . . and that you can help them reach that goal.
2. Evaluate your fellow stakeholders' commitment to all students becoming joyful, independent readers and writers.
3. Demonstrate your commitment through action.

We know that each step is hard work, requiring deep reflection. Keep these steps (and the reflections you collected in this chapter's two templates) in focus as we proceed through the next five chapters.

Rose: *I remember my own first steps on this journey. A few years ago, I was called into the associate superintendent's office and handed a stack of printouts eight inches high. As the associate superintendent handed me the heavy load, he said, "Our board members are concerned about suspensions* *at the middle schools. Pull a group of our best middle school teachers and administrators together and come up with a plan."*

Not delighted with the assignment, I began to look at the data on these students. I was excited to discover that all the middle school students who had been suspended 30 days or more were reading below the 25th percentile on the Stanford Achievement Test. This gave me the justification I needed to recommend we develop a literacy intervention plan, rather than a discipline plan. With the support of the district leadership, we formed a committee that did just that, but there were many who doubted our approach. One of these was the district evaluator I asked to research the project. His comment: "Don't you know that if students get to middle school and can't read, you can't teach them?"

Well, the researcher was wrong. When our design was implemented, he documented exceptional gains in reading on a number of measures. I'll never forget the researcher's words, 12 months later, when he delivered his evaluation report to the superintendent: "I am embarrassed and ashamed for ever thinking these students couldn't learn to read. They were never the problem. The problem was always us."

We urge you to make that commitment today. Commit yourself to literacy leadership—to becoming the solution and not the problem. Commit yourself to all students in your school being joyful, independent readers and writers. Commit yourself to a system of fail-safe literacy.

Further reading in literacy and leadership

Atwell, N. (1998). *In the middle: New understandings about writing, reading, and learning* (2nd ed.). Portsmouth, NH: Boynton/Cook.

Beers, K., & Samuels, B. G. (1998). *Into focus: Understanding and creating middle school readers.* Norwood, MA: Christopher-Gordon Publishers.

Blase, J., & Blase, J. (1998). *Handbook of instructional leadership: How really good principals promote teaching and learning.* Thousand Oaks, CA: Corwin.

Blase, J., & Blase, J. (2001). *Empowering teachers: What successful principals do.* Thousand Oaks, CA: Corwin.

Blasewitz, M., & Taylor, R. (1999, January). Attacking literacy with technology in an urban setting. *Middle School Journal, 30*(3), 33–39.

Brown, J. L., & Moffett, C. A. (1999). *The hero's journey: How educators can transform schools and improve learning.* Alexandria, VA: Association for Supervision and Curriculum Development.

Daniels, H., Bizar, M., & Zemelman, S. (2001). *Rethinking high school: Best practice in teaching, learning, and leadership.* Portsmouth, NH: Heinemann.

Hargreaves, A. (Ed.). (1997). *Rethinking educational change with heart and mind: 1997 ASCD yearbook.* Alexandria, VA: Association for Supervision and Curriculum Development.

Hasselbring, T. S., Goin, L., Taylor, R., Bottge, B., & Daley, P. (1997, November). The computer doesn't embarrass me. *Educational Leadership, 55*(3), 30–33.

Jensen, E. (1998). *Teaching with the brain in mind.* Alexandria, VA: Association for Supervision and Curriculum Development.

Lambert, L. (1998). *Building leadership capacity in schools.* Alexandria, VA: Association for Supervision and Curriculum Development.

Marsh, D. D. (Ed.). (1999). *Preparing our schools for the 21st century: 1999 ASCD yearbook.* Alexandria, VA: Association for Supervision and Curriculum Development.

Patton, S., & Holmes, M. (Eds.). (1998). *The keys to literacy.* Washington, DC: Council for Basic Education.

Sergiovanni, T. J. (1996). *Leadership for the schoolhouse: How is it different? Why is it important?* San Francisco: Jossey-Bass Publishers.

Smith, W. F., & Andrews, R. L. (1989). *Instructional leadership: How principals make a dif-.ference.* Alexandria, VA: Association for Supervision and Curriculum Development.

Sprenger, M. (1999). *Learning and memory: The brain in action.* Alexandria, VA: Association for Supervision and Curriculum Development.

Taylor, R. (1999, December). Missing pieces: Aligned curriculum, instruction, and assessment. *Schools in the Middle, 9*(4), 14–16.

Taylor, R. (2001, October). Steps to literacy. *Principal Leadership, 2*(2), 34–39.

Wilson, E. (1999). *Reading at the middle and high school levels: Building active readers across the curriculum.* Arlington, VA: Educational Research Service.

2

Using Data to Design a System of Literacy

YOU'VE MADE THE COMMITMENT TO PROVIDE LITERACY LEADERSHIP SO THAT ALL students in your school will become joyful, independent readers and writers. In your actions, stakeholders will see evidence of your belief in them and the students, and they will join you in developing the fail-safe system of literacy for your school. Now it's time to turn to the hard work of designing that system.

Principals often comment to us that their students are reading more since the implementation of a motivational reading program. Our response is always a request for more information. "*Who* is reading more and who isn't?" The answer is almost always that "good readers," the high-achieving students, are reading more . . . and that poorer readers still aren't reading. To set up a fail-safe system that helps *all* students become joyful, independent readers and writers—and you can—you must begin by examining the status quo. The critical question to answer is this: Which of your students—as individuals and as groups—are currently learning literacy behaviors satisfactorily and which are not?

First, some terminology and background. "Literacy behaviors" are the use of literacy processes: reading, writing, listening, speaking, viewing, and thinking. By middle and high school, many students have learned literacy behaviors well and can go about their classwork and homework independently, applying reading, writing, listening, and so forth as necessary to complete each task they encounter. Other middle and high school students are just getting by . . . and have difficulty discovering factual, much less inferential, information in textbooks or in classroom discussions.

As the leader, you must use all your skills and knowledge to help stakeholders examine how your school is serving students now, reflect on how to serve students better, and then make better decisions about your daily work. Careful examination of *individual* student data will help ensure informed decision making about the effectiveness of current policies and which specific *groups* of students your literacy system should target and measure. For example, a school with a motivational reading program benefiting only good readers might modify the program's implementation so that participation doesn't academically punish poor readers. The school might also add a more appropriate independent reading experience for struggling students. New practices and policies like these will result in positive changes in student achievement.

The task of identifying who is learning literacy behaviors satisfactorily and who is not is too complicated for the principal to take on alone, as the information you gather may need in-depth discussion, may be controversial, or may be uncomfortable to face. In our experience, working with a collaborative Literacy Leadership Team—made up of administrators and teachers across grade-levels and content areas—makes the process easier. Together, you will need to work through the following four steps:

1. Identify the data and evidence that you will accept.
2. Gather and analyze the acceptable data and evidence.
3. Identify, prioritize, and target individual students and groups of students for literacy outreach.
4. Identify, prioritize, and target individual teachers and groups of teachers for literacy-related coaching.

Let's examine the steps, one by one.

Step 1: Identify the data and evidence that you will accept

To kick off your examination of who is learning literacy behaviors and who is not, decide which data and evidence that you and your staff will accept as meaningful in your unique school community. In this context, *data* refers to test scores, grade profiles, and other official information used to quantify and describe a school or the achievement of its students. *Evidence* tends to be closer to the classroom and refers to student work and observations of student and teacher behavior, attitudes, and culture.

You will want to consider a variety of data ranging from standardized test data to demographic data on students and the professional staff. Such data will provide insight into who the students and staff are and how their learning needs may be approached. For instance, if 25 percent of students are learning English as a second language or if 40 percent are on free and reduced lunch, this information can be valuable in designing home-school communication on literacy. Other factors you may choose to investigate are student and teacher mobility rates, the number of students with disabilities (physical or cognitive), and absentee rates of students and staff. From this data, you can generate summary profiles of students and faculty.

Figure 2.1 provides an example of a student summary profile. Without digging deeper into the data, we can generalize from this kind of summary that XYZ Middle School needs literacy learning and that to be successful, the program must incorporate materials and strategies appropriate for older students. Home-school relationship development related to literacy learning may also be important. The school would proceed from this summary to a closer look to determine which specific students are priorities for literacy intervention.

EXAMPLE

FIGURE 2.1
A Student Summary Profile

At XYZ Middle School

❖   25% of students are enrolled in the English as a Second Language program. These students' home language is generally Spanish or Creole, and parents do not speak English proficiently.

❖   40% of students qualify for free or reduced lunch.

❖   10% of the 300 students in 8th grade have been retained twice previously and are approaching 16 years of age. Most of these students are male.

Identifying sources of evidence

Let's think about the meaningful evidence related to literacy achievement that you might find within your school. Some might be generated by students on standardized tests, but the great majority is generated by students on classroom work. Begin with what evidences are available on who is and who is not learning literacy behaviors satisfactorily. Then ask, "What evidences do we have on *how* specific students are learning literacy behaviors?" Possible sources of this evidence include the following.

Book circulation records in the media center. Who checks out which books? Who never checks out books? What books are most interesting to students? This evidence will help shed light on reading levels and clarify the type and quantity of books your school should consider ordering.

Reading opportunities in the classroom. Which classrooms encourage independent reading? How often? What percentage of students read independently when given the opportunity? What is the size of classroom libraries? What selections can be found in classroom libraries? This evidence will let you know which teachers value independent reading and what classroom practices are working.

Required reading in the classroom. What are the required readings in classes? How do teachers ensure that all students can and do read these pieces? Requiring reading is a positive step; knowing who reads the required books is even more important. By identifying teachers who assist every student in accessing required reading, you gain additional insight into commitment levels and effective practices.

Writing opportunities in the classroom. Are writing portfolios available for students? Are there writing centers in classrooms? Are samples of student writing posted for celebration? Identifying writing opportunities—particularly those that go beyond preparation for mandated writing tests—can indicate the degree to which your curriculum (and your teachers) incorporate literacy processes.

Student performance on unit tests. What does the grade profile look like for unit tests? Which students consistently do well on these assessments and which consistently do not? Are reading and writing required for satisfactory performance? Remember that performance on end-of-unit tests reflects the extent to which the content taught was tested. Alignment of curriculum, instruction, learning tools, and assessment is important to making gains in literacy learning.

Student performance on commercial software activities and assessments. Who does well on software activities and assessments, but not on pencil-and-paper assignments? Such evidence will show which students' strengths lie either with the use of technology or traditional educational media, providing information on how best to assist them with literacy learning.

Student performance in visual or performing arts. Who shines when asked to demonstrate what they know through the visual or performing arts, but not on pencil-and-paper tasks? Knowing who can demonstrate what they have learned through the arts tells you where to begin with their literacy learning.

Student grades. Which students are getting *As, Bs, Cs, Ds,* or *Fs*? Are there other ways that low-performing students are showing they have literacy learning needs? Do the low-performing students shine in other ways? Developing profiles for students will clarify trends in their learning that will guide improvement in schoolwide literacy. Most school literacy teams will be able to identify the artistically or musically talented students who do not do well on content area teacher-made tests. Often, these same students demonstrate deep knowledge when they're allowed to do so by using their other talents.

This list is intended to start your thinking about what *you* will accept as evidence of literacy in your school. Ultimately, only you and your staff members are qualified to make this determination. After generating a list of potential sources of evidence, you and your Literacy Leadership Team should select the evidences that have meaning for your particular school setting. The first year, perhaps the team will select "safe" evidence perceived to be nonthreatening; the second year, they might select evidence closer to the teachers. In any event, allowing the team to select what is meaningful is empowering and helps to ensure that everyone will pay attention to what is found. The bottom line is that your school has a wealth of evidence on student performance and on how teachers are addressing literacy learning. Considering literacy information from these sources will give you a richer picture of the opportunities for improving literacy that are already available in your school and a clearer idea of which students these measures target. You will also discover which individuals and groups of individuals are falling outside the scope of current measures and which are simply not taking advantage of opportunities available to them.

For example, one opportunity for literacy learning might be the availability of a commercial software program (such as Renaissance Learning's Accelerated Reader or Scholastic's Reading Counts) that allows students to take a 10-question quiz on a book they have just read and receive immediate feedback on their quiz performance. Students who read the most books and earn satisfactory scores on the quizzes might receive prizes, awards, and recognition. A Literacy Leadership Team looking at the data on who receives these awards should investigate if this data is consistent with other literacy data on the same students. Are the students who *never* receive awards or who never take advantage of this opportunity the same students who need to build fluency in reading? As one principal said to us recently, "Yes, we have independent reading for all of our students; in fact, there's a software program in the media center that really motivates students to read. On the other hand, I guess those who really need to improve their reading don't take advantage of this motivational program."

Our experience mirrors this principal's. Students who read and write below grade level are less likely to take advantage of optional literacy learning opportunities that already exist, and they benefit from having expectations and accountability set for them. Depending on what you find in your own school, you may end up changing current "opportunities" for literacy learning into expectations for all students.

Identifying evidence of who is learning literacy behaviors satisfactorily and who is not makes a lot of sense, because this evidence is observable in our school environments every day. This collection of evidences is how we know what we know. Before reading on, take some time to intentionally select the evidence that you will consider in developing your fail-safe system of literacy.

Identifying sources of data

In this period of accountability, most principals already spend quite a bit of time looking at the results of standardized test data, particularly the mean, median, and mode percentiles for reading comprehension, vocabulary, and writing. We invite you to look at the data in more detail than you have done before and use that analysis to guide your literacy program planning and decisions. Depending on your school's resources, you might enlist the support of a testing expert or research analyst to identify data sources and to help disaggregate the data (see Step 2, page 28).

Begin by brainstorming the data sources available to you. These sources encompass "normative data"—that is, student performance on standardized tests. Other data sources may include reading tests used in the classroom, such as those in the Degrees of Reading Power (DRP) program or Scholastic Reading Inventory (SRI). Student performance data on the Preliminary Scholastic Assessment Test (PSAT), Scholastic Assessment Test (SAT), and American College Test (ACT) are also good sources of verbal and mathematical reasoning and content performance data, which are all related to literacy behaviors. Other data to consider include student failure rates, retention rates, average number of credits earned per year, and multi-year comparison data on student groupings. The following subsections provide more detail on each of these data categories.

Normative data. This data on student literacy levels may come from large-scale assessments such as the Iowa Tests of Basic Skills or the California Achievement Test and from state tests, like the Texas Assessment of Academic Skills (TAAS) or the Florida Comprehensive Assessment Test (FCAT). Some districts have their own locally developed tests tied to district curriculum or classroom assessments. The normative data we're concerned with is usually generated from language arts assessments, which, whether large-scale (e.g., Iowa) or district-customized, measure reading comprehension, vocabulary, mechanics, and writing.

In addition to the data from basic tests, you will want to examine data from subtests such as those that measure students' ability to construct meaning from informational texts and from literature. We worked with an Alabama school district that was perplexed to learn that although its middle school students do well on mechanics of language, they do poorly on comprehension and writing. This type of difference in subtest scores is common. Students can learn mechanics through direct instruction and practice, but writing and reading comprehension are much higher-level literacy processes that develop through modeling and guided and independent practice. By incorporating literacy processes into daily classroom activities, and by incorporating reading strategies before, during, and after reading throughout the school day, both writing and reading comprehension will improve. The greatest gains in reading comprehension will occur when schools also incorporate accountable independent reading every day. Chapter 4 discusses classrooms for literacy learning in more depth.

We also suggest you look beyond language arts assessment results. Examining data from standardized *content* tests, such as those for mathematics, social studies, and science, will reveal content reading strengths and difficulties that your fail-safe system of literacy may address. For example, in mathematics you may learn that mean scores in computation are higher than mean scores in problem solving, suggesting difficulties in comprehension. Data from social studies and science subtests shed light on students' facility with vocabulary and concepts and their fluency reading and understanding nonfiction. Improvement in students' reading and writing will enhance their performance on all content assessments.

Classroom data. Data that teachers use as tools for instructional decision making, like the DRP, the SRI, or the San Diego Quick Assessment provide valuable, readily accessible information on student growth in reading comprehension. With this data from two or three dates during the school year, you can quickly determine the growth of individual students and groups of students.

Other classroom data sources you might find interesting include sample writing portfolios, performance-based assessments (including technology and media work samples), and rubrics demonstrating growth or lack of growth over a period of time. You will think of other data sources that are available in your classrooms that will confirm or dispel notions you have about literacy learning.

Student grouping data. Reviewing data on the number of students in each level of instructional groupings your school uses will provide you with another perspective on student literacy performance. Often, students are recommended for levels based on reading comprehension data. How many students are in above-average or college-bound classes? How many are in average-level classes? How many students are grouped in a lower-performing category? Over a period of several years, what trends can you detect in the numbers and percentages of students by race and gender in each level? Looking at trend data will shed light on teachers' perceptions of student performance and help you set priorities for literacy learning that, over time, will lead to more students' inclusion in higher-level classes.

Other types of grouping data you may find helpful relate to students receiving special services. For example, how many students in your school receive second-language instruction in English? Once enrolled, how long do they continue to participate in these classes? What percentage of your English language learners transition to non-ESL language arts and content courses? How successful are they, and do they graduate from high school? Nationally, this is an at-risk population that needs to be closely studied and well supported. If your ESL population is significant, you have an important opportunity to affect students' lives through development of literacy behaviors.

Another example of special services groupings that can generate data on who is learning literacy behaviors satisfactorily and who is not are the nontraditional instructional opportunities, such as before-school interventions, during-school interventions, and after-school interventions. Look carefully at indicators of growth to determine what specific learning experiences are supporting students. Nontraditional programs may take place on the school campus or in community centers, Boys and Girls Clubs, or churches.

You may also want to review the literacy achievement of traditionally under-performing groups in your school (categorized by ethnicity, economic conditions, the language students speak at home, or other criteria unique to your school). The purpose of disaggregating data for these students is not to identify students who "cannot achieve," but to ensure that the program you design will meet their needs. Being sure that high expectations, high standards, and opportunities are communicated to all students lays the foundation for higher levels of literacy learning. For historically underperforming groups, it is important to chart their growth over time to make sure that the achievement gap continues to close.

Consider these potential data sources and make a list of those you want to study. Once you've done this, you and your team will be ready to gather and analyze evidence and data to learn who is learning literacy behaviors satisfactorily and who is not.

Step 2: Gather and analyze the acceptable data and evidence

It may take weeks to gather the data and evidence that you have determined to be acceptable. Set up a collection system that is simple to access and duplicate. One suggestion is to put all data and evidence in cartons with file folders that are clearly marked. Most data will be available electronically or will be in an existing school profile.

The actual evidence gathering will take a bit of planning. We suggest having a single designee issue a request for information to faculty and staff, being sure to pinpoint exactly what evidence is to be supplied and how it will be used. (This clarity is critical in minimizing staff anxiety.) Once the evidence is in, the designee should summarize it and prepare a report for the Literacy Leadership Team. In larger schools, evidence may be gathered and organized by academic teams, grade levels, or academic departments.

Once all data and evidence are gathered, it's a good idea to enter the findings in a database. If this is not possible, a notebook with a table of contents and sections for each data source and evidence source will suffice. You or your designee may need to prepare several notebooks' worth of this data and evidence for your Literacy Leadership Team.

During the data and evidence-gathering phase, it will be natural for discussions, reflection, and professional insight to take place. You'll find that some of the data and evidence will begin to take on greater meaning. Don't feel compelled to use *all* that you have gathered! Before starting the analysis, we encourage you to determine which of the meaningful evidence and data you've gathered will be *most helpful* for developing an overview of the school and setting priorities for your system of fail-safe literacy. For instance, you may determine that to develop a complete picture of literacy behaviors in your school, you will need to consider standardized test data, information on student attendance, and teachers' grade profiles related to the test data (a comparison of students' scores on standardized test and their classroom grades). You may also decide that you will review achievement performance of special populations, for example students in intervention programs, ESL programs, or exceptional education programs.

After thoughtfully deciding which data sources and evidence will provide you with the most insight on who is learning literacy behaviors satisfactorily and who is not, design a graphic representation of the data you have collected. In this graphic, you may want to include information that affects who is learning, like attendance or mobility data. First, decide which views will be most helpful in making decisions. You'll probably want to show whole-school views that include school median percentiles and numbers of students performing in each quartile. You may also want to show grade-level views that mirror the whole-school view. Some grades may have standardized test data and others may not, so be sure to build in cells or columns that include all the information you consider valuable.

Besides analysis by grades, we encourage you to think in terms of smaller units, such as classes, for both language arts and content areas. You may find that students in certain language classes do well on the writing assessment, but that the same students fail miserably when asked to write on a mathematics assessment or science assessment. If the same students perform well in one content area and poorly in another, this indicates a need to focus on literacy behaviors in that content area and a need to read and write more nonfiction in the language arts class.

Looking carefully at data collected on special populations—such as students who have been retained, students enrolled in special education or ESL programs, and students who have been enrolled in your school for less than one year—will provide excellent information on the level of effectiveness of literacy instruction there. By continuing to break the data down into different, smaller groups, you will probably see a pattern emerging that will provide you with clear targets for improving literacy behaviors.

For example, a few years ago we were searching the systemwide data, looking for patterns that would provide insight to improving student literacy learning. The profile we found was this: Students who had been in enrolled in the *same* school for four years prior to the standardized assessment had a mean reading comprehension score in the 60th percentile (above grade level), regardless of the school. Students who did not qualify for the free or reduced lunch program had a mean score in the 60th percentile regardless of the school. Students who moved during the period preceding standardized assessment scored similarly to those students on free and reduced lunch. We concluded that mobility was a highly influential factor in these scores, which we could not impact directly, but could impact by viewing the issue not as one of mobility, but one of providing equitable access to a curriculum of high standards across the district. The action generated was to provide consistency among schools (alignment) to minimize the negative impact of mobility. Another approach might be to intervene with a "jump start" program for transferred students, much like some schools do for students who have recently emigrated.

Before you can come to such conclusions—and take such actions—you need to organize student achievement data for analysis. This can be tricky. We can recommend three models for doing so. A thorough study of your school's data would use all three models for the specific population that you serve.

Model 1: An overview of whole-school student performance by grade level for one academic year

Typically, schools compare a given grade level's performance during one year to its performance the next year. Aside from the obvious benefits of helping you compare one group's performance to another, this model is a particularly effective means of gauging the impact of significant changes in personnel, curriculum, instruction, or professional development. See Figure 2.2 for a sample template. In developing your own data-gathering template, you will need to determine the features that distinguish your school in literacy learning. As you see, Figure 2.2 is organized to allow the school to compare data by gender, grade-level, ethnicity, second-language status, and socioeconomic status. Recently, teachers in one of the schools we were working with noted a drop in the mean percentile in the 7th grade—a drop that cut across other features as well. They noted that within the school, 7th graders were also the most likely to be retained. As a group, the 7th grade teachers took action and went on to infuse literacy learning in all content areas.

TEMPLATE

FIGURE 2.2
Overview of Whole-School Performance

Sub-groups	Grade levels	Quartile 1		Quartile 2		Quartile 3		Quartile 4	
		Males	Females	Males	Females	Males	Females	Males	Females
Ethnicity	Grade ____								
	Grade ____								
	Grade ____								
Language	Grade ____								
	Grade ____								
	Grade ____								
Poverty	Grade ____								
	Grade ____								
	Grade ____								

Model 2: A comparison of a given student population's performance over time

It may be more helpful to follow a cohort of students from one grade level to the next (for example, follow the 5th grade reading comprehension mean percentile to the 6th grade, to the 7th grade, and to the 8th grade). If the percentile remains steady, the students are demonstrating typical growth for their grade level each year. If there is a downward trend in the percentile, the students are losing ground; conversely, if the percentile shows steady growth, the students are learning more than their peers nationally and are closing the achievement gap! See Figure 2.3 for an example of this model. As the figure shows, you can subdivide data on student cohorts by gender, race, socioeconomic status, and so on, to determine who is learning more and make better decisions about intervention targeted at specific subgroups.

EXAMPLE

FIGURE 2.3
A Comparison of a Given Student Population's Performance

Reading Comprehension Scores

School Year	Grade	Median Percentile
1997	5th	36
1998	6th	38
1999	7th	42
2000	8th	44
2001	9th	45

Model 3: A comparison of individual students' performance

After reviewing data for the whole school broken down into smaller units, you may want to create a profile of individual students. You may have the resources to develop a profile on every student or to take an in-depth look at specific populations. We recommend that you at least identify every student performing in the lower quartile in reading comprehension, vocabulary, writing, and mathematics. As the template in Figure 2.4 suggests, for individual student analysis, you may choose to look at the same

TEMPLATE

FIGURE 2.4
Comparison of Individual Students' Performance

Directions: Use this chart to record data gathered for a targeted group of students at the beginning, middle, and end of the year or as a chart to record data for an entire class.

Student Name	Reading Compre-hension Percentile	Vocabulary Percentile	Writing Percentile	Mathematics Percentile	Portfolio Assessment	Other

data and add evidence from portfolio assessments or other indicators such as projects, media center records, and technology programs. Looking at individual student data will help you develop richer profiles with more concrete evidence of performance or lack of performance. These profiles will help you clarify what may be needed or at least which students need targeted support.

In addition, although it's a potentially sensitive move, you may also choose to gather and analyze data on the performance of classes assigned to individual teachers or groups of teachers. For example, within the particular grade levels or content areas you're investigating, how do each teacher's classes perform? An isolated dip in performance can be explained away. (All administrators are aware that the frequent absence of a teacher or a series of long-term substitutes can lower a group of students' achievement in a given school year.) Remember that to draw meaningful implications, you will need to compare students' classroom performance data at the beginning of the year with their performance data at the end of the year. Looking at data on the growth in learning of students served by the same teacher for several years will provide you with valuable insight on students' literacy growth.

Step 3: Identify, prioritize, and target individual students and groups of students for literacy outreach

After you have gathered and analyzed the data on student performance, it will be easier for you to determine the priorities for your literacy program. Think about which group or groups of students you want to begin with. Perhaps it's the 6th grade students in language arts or those students entering middle school reading below the 40th percentile. Or you may want to start with 8th grade students across all content areas, particularly if your district or state targets 8th graders for large-scale, accountability-focused assessment or grade-level retention.

Frequently, high school literacy programs prioritize the 9th grade, as that grade is usually the one with the highest number of retentions and is traditionally viewed as "the last chance for success" before students drop out. You may also choose to target high-performing measurements like SAT or Advanced Placement enrollments or exam results. Setting priorities helps to improve literacy learning for all students. In our experience, when teachers incorporate literacy processes and strategies to assist targeted groups, the success they experience often motivates them to use the same results-oriented strategies with the rest of the class.

For decision-making and planning purposes related to literacy learning, we encourage you to assign priority rankings to the individual students and the groups of students. Use a scale from one to five, with one being the highest priority and five being the lowest priority (although still an important one). As the individuals and groups are prioritized, you and your Literacy Leadership Team should brainstorm various ways to serve these students better. Write down your ideas so that you don't forget them, but don't jump to planning yet. You will use these priorities in the following chapters as you create your fail-safe system of literacy.

Step 4: Identify, prioritize, and target individual teachers and groups of teachers for literacy-related coaching

We administrators help students by helping teachers to teach more effectively. From this perspective, it makes sense to identify how well teachers are affecting student learning. For literacy learning to improve, professional educators must change what they teach, how they teach, how they assess, what learning tools they use, and perhaps even the classroom environment they create.

When you look at the students you are targeting, also think about who their teachers are. If you decide your middle school literacy efforts will focus on 6th grade (as the transition grade to middle school) or on 8th grade (because of state or district assessments at that level), then you will also need to focus on the groups of teachers that work with these students. Furthermore, you must decide which teachers in those groups are the highest priorities for professional development opportunities and list them. Begin with the groups of students prioritized, identify the teachers affecting the literacy learning of these students, and group the teachers in priority order from one to five. Again, this prioritization does not reflect teachers' effectiveness; rather it reflects their students' needs. If we use the example of prioritizing 6th grade students, then a Literacy Leadership Team may prioritize teacher targets like this:

1 = 6th grade language arts teachers
2 = 6th grade mathematics teachers
3 = 6th grade science and social studies teachers
4 = 6th grade electives teachers
5 = 6th grade special education teachers

What can help you deal with the sensitive issue of how to address individual teacher performance? Once you have looked at an individual teacher's data over time, then you will have the kind of evidence you'll need to work with that teacher on improvement. Depending on the evidence, the culture of the school, the political environment, and other factors, it may be advisable to prioritize these teachers confidentially. If only one teacher is working with a particular group of students (as would be the case in a small school or perhaps for AP English), targeting that particular teacher would not be as sensitive an issue, and supporting that teacher's improvement in daily work may be more readily accepted.

In the Classroom

Just a few weeks before the start of a new school year, Tony Watlington was hired as the new principal of James B. Dudley High School in Greensboro, North Carolina. An instructional leader with a clear vision for literacy, Tony hit the ground running. The first thing on his agenda was identifying data his Literacy Leadership Team would use to create a fail-safe system of literacy. The work was soon underway, with the team screening vast amounts of data to determine what evidence would be acceptable. Their list of data included a site analysis, end-of-course and end-of-grade scores on state norm-referenced exams, and the San Diego Quick Assessment (to identify reading levels), along with comparative data based on the school's academic standing in the district.

The site analysis provided foundational information that compared Dudley High School's past history with the current status of its student population, demographics, and discipline and attendance rates, along with students' reading levels by quartile over the past five years. This was an initial snapshot of who was learning literacy behaviors satisfactorily and who was not. Results of an academic trend study from 1994 to 2001 targeted the percentage of students scoring in the lower quartiles. Tony and his team compared this data to student performance in core subjects across Guilford County Schools. These findings showed that the smallest gap between Dudley High School's average and the Guilford County School District's average occurred in 1994 in the areas of biology, U.S. history, and chemistry. Having identified the time period when the school's achievement was more closely aligned with other schools in the district, they could begin to explore what had changed at Dudley since that time.

Tony and his team didn't stop there. They decided to use standardized test data from the North Carolina End of Course (EOC) and End of Grade (EOG) assessments to further clarify who was learning and who was not. The next step was to determine the group of students to be targeted for improvement. It was obvious from the team's findings that the students who were unsuccessful with the state exams and who most often read below the 50th percentile would be the focus of their literacy efforts. Students were given the San Diego Quick Assessment to determine reading levels.

Once the target students had been identified, the team turned their attention to teacher selection. Who would teach these students? Who would believe in them and persevere in a vision of excellence for reluctant readers? Initially, a select group of language arts teachers took on the task, working with students across grade levels. In the coming year, James B. Dudley High School plans to fine-tune its approach with a specialized team of teachers in a 9th grade school-within-a-school concept. The target will be incoming 9th grade students reading below the 50th percentile.

The final use of the data was to direct and design professional development. The team selected a comprehensive research-based reading process as a framework to focus on the systematic and explicit approach to instruction. Renee McKinnon, the former curriculum facilitator at Dudley High School, served as an in-house support for teachers, providing resources, training, and encouragement. Professional development dates were set, along with ongoing meetings to discuss what the evidence was showing them about who was learning literacy behaviors satisfactorily and who was not.

The time and effort Tony Watlington and his team invested in data identification, gathering, and alignment will mean a valuable reward. They are creating literacy-focused classrooms and improving student achievement, and they are moving ever closer to their end goal—for all students at Dudley High School to become joyful, independent readers and writers.

Review and reflection

Gathering and studying the data has taken you weeks—time you thought you couldn't spare from the daily operation of the school. Already, you're starting to see positive results as you work closely with your Literacy Leadership Team. Both you and these stakeholders now know much more about who in your school is learning literacy behaviors satisfactorily and who is not. Much of the data has informed team members about the performance of their colleagues, and they have practiced handling this information professionally and confidentially.

With the knowledgeable, collegial support you now have and the priorities that have been established, your Literacy Leadership Team will have a more informed approach to working on curriculum alignment, creating a classroom for literacy, professional development, and building capacity. As you read the following chapters, keep the data and priorities in mind. The priorities will indicate the discrepancies for initial focus in Chapter 3. They will provide evidence for making decisions that will help you lead your school to a fail-safe system of literacy.

Further reading in using data in literacy leadership

Schmoker, M. (1999). *Results: The key to continuous school improvement* (2nd ed.). Alexandria, VA: Association for Supervision and Curriculum Development.

Schmoker, M. (2001). *The results fieldbook: Practical strategies from dramatically improved schools*. Alexandria, VA: Association for Supervision and Curriculum Development.

3

Aligning Curriculum, Instruction, Learning Tools, and Assessment

---

To many school leaders, creating a curriculum system of aligned curriculum, instruction, learning tools, and assessment may sound like an esoteric exercise that has little to do with real school practice. But this task takes on significant meaning when we view it as a way to provide school leadership for streamlining and simplifying the work of teachers, while also ensuring that all students have equal access to a high-quality curriculum. This equal access results from an officially aligned curriculum, available to all students, and from daily, schoolwide incorporation of literacy processes and strategies that will help all students to learn that curriculum.

When all students have this kind of equal access, both achievement and standardized test results will improve. An aligned curriculum system will also result in more efficient and effective daily teaching. It will make it easier for teachers to create meaningful integrated (or "problem-based") learning by bundling standards. Finally, the enhanced curricular and instructional practices that follow alignment will help more students become joyful, independent readers and writers.

In the United States, almost all states and most school districts have now developed required curriculum for all content areas taught in each grade level, complete with specific standards and sets of benchmarks. Many states and districts have also identified indicators of performance for each standard so that teachers will know what to look for in students' work. In elementary schools, these indicators are often set for each grade level. In middle school, the standards, benchmarks, and performance indicators tend to span grades 6–8, and in high school, grades 9–12. Three-quarters of the states use mandatory tests to provide an extra incentive to teach the state-designated standards.

This big picture approach to curriculum is necessary, but it does little to help school leadership enhance literacy learning for all students. The good news is that with the state and district curriculum in hand and a thorough understanding of the data on student performance in his or her school, the fail-safe literacy leader is equipped to create a curriculum system of aligned curriculum, instruction through literacy, learning tools, and assessment where it matters most—in the classroom.

In working through the process of creating an aligned system with your teachers and Literacy Leadership Team, use the following six questions to guide you:

1. What do you want your students to know and be able to do related to literacy learning?
2. What literacy strategies work best with your students and what other, research-based strategies do you want to use?
3. Do both classroom and standardized assessments reflect actual classroom practice?
4. Do the learning tools in your school support the curriculum, instructional strategies, and assessments?
5. How will you eliminate unproductive practices?
6. How will you know that your curriculum system is aligned?

Answering these questions will take varying amounts of time, depending upon the level of collaboration that already exists among the teachers in your school and the present extent of alignment. As you and your staff consider the questions and ultimately reach a schoolwide consensus on the answers, use the template in Figure 3.1 as a tool to record and compare the current status of alignment ("What Is . . .") and the desired status ("What Should Be . . ."). Now, let's examine each of the critical questions, addressing the issues you and your staff should expect to address.

TEMPLATE

FIGURE 3.1
Curriculum System Alignment Chart

System Component	What Is ...	What Should Be ...
Curriculum		
Instructional Strategies		
Learning Tools		
Assessment		
Professional Development		

Question 1: What do you want your students to know and be able to do related to literacy learning?

Before we jump into this question, let's first try to take some of the mystique out of curriculum. Generally, curriculum is written in subject-specific strands of processes, concepts, knowledge, or skills that begin at a specific grade level and continue through another specific grade level. In a subject like language arts, many strands extend from kindergarten through 12th grade, addressing various aspects of reading, writing, listening, viewing, speaking, language, and literature.

Obviously, literacy behaviors—the *processes* of reading, writing, speaking, listening, viewing, and thinking—are often the subject of specific language arts standards, especially in the early grades. But it's also clear that literacy behaviors are necessary in all content areas and at all grade levels. They are the tools students use to access knowledge and communicate what they have learned (which is why it's so essential that students work on them throughout the school day). High-performing teachers regularly incorporate each of these literacy processes in their instructional plans to help students develop both the vocabulary related to a particular unit of study and an overall comprehension of that curriculum.

For this reason, we believe that when you and your staff begin your curriculum alignment by responding to the question of what you want your students to know and be able to do, you should focus on literacy processes—reading, writing, speaking, listening, viewing, and thinking—regardless of the content area. This will help you create successful solutions for meeting diverse student learning needs across *all* content areas.

In answering this first critical question, teachers should not develop a "wish list" of every last thing that they would like their students to learn, but identify just what is *essential*. Ideally, these "essential learnings" should be at least a subset of the standards for your district and state. Depending on your students, it is possible that you and your teachers may identify as essential some things that are not included in your official curriculum. However, most official curricula are so broad that you probably will be able to identify essential learnings for your students from among the items on the official list.

Understanding that standards and benchmarks develop on a continuum through 12 or 13 grades and vary only a little from year to year should help to simplify the process of identifying essential learnings. Let's look at some examples. In the lower grades, a standard in the strand of reading may be to "select simple reference materials (such as a picture book) to gain information." By middle school, the standard may be to "use a variety of reference materials and technology to obtain information for a research project." The essential, literacy-related learnings in both of these standards are that students are able to read, write, view, and think. Likewise, a 5th grade mathematics standard in the strand of communication may be to "read a word problem and select correct operations to solve the problem." By 8th or 9th grade, the standard may require students to "read the word problem and explain how to solve it."

Through our experience developing curriculum, we've learned that many teachers see their teaching as a series of activities, rather than a 10-month process for reaching long-term goals that will position students for the start of the next grade-level's 10-month process.

> **Rose:** *When working with teachers on our district's curriculum redesign project, I found that most had favorite units that they enjoyed teaching and didn't want to give up—even if these units were not in the official curriculum and were not measured on state and district tests. When working with your teachers on curriculum alignment, you may also run into this problem and wonder how you will address it. I found myself listening to these teachers and very often replying, "If you think your students need to know about that topic, please teach it after they have mastered the grade-level expectations and have taken the mandated test. Or find a way to teach the grade-level expectations through your favorite unit."*

As this example shows, there is a fine balance between ensuring that all students have access to the same high-quality curriculum and instruction and empowering teachers to be creative and do their best work.

We encourage you to ask your teachers to study the data on student achievement (see Chapter 2) and then identify the essential learnings (standards and benchmarks) for your student population. Then you and the teachers will be ready to discuss instructional planning to incorporate literacy processes and strategies. Otherwise, you may end up with wonderfully creative units that do not have a direct relationship to data-driven literacy needs or to official curriculum and assessment.

Question 2: What literacy strategies work best with your students and what other, research-based strategies do you want to use?

Once you've identified your students' essential learnings, you're ready to explore the means to achieve these goals. The literature on adolescent literacy is clear that student achievement improves when literacy strategies are explicitly taught to students and are used regularly to provide them with opportunities to comprehend text in both language arts and content classes. Literacy strategies are typically grouped into three categories, reflecting how teachers use them:

❖ *Before-reading strategies*—such as anticipation guides, read-alouds, and art and music activities—engage students' interest and help them to access prior knowledge.

❖ *During-reading strategies*—such as completing reading guides, making predictions about what will happen next, or using sticky notes to write questions about the reading—help students to comprehend what they are reading by deepening understanding and linking one part of the reading to the next.

❖ *After-reading strategies*—such as drawing relationships to another text, to students' lives, to their prior knowledge, and to the world beyond school—help students find relevance in the reading and support retention.

If your Literacy Leadership Team does not have expertise in literacy strategies, do some research in this area to find out which ones are likely to work best in your environment. Chapter 4 provides more insight into middle and high school classrooms where all students are succeeding with meaningful, challenging work as a result of deliberate inclusion of literacy strategies.

Once literacy strategies have been selected—and learned—teachers will be ready to develop instructional plans that use the agreed-upon strategies to address the identified standards and benchmarks. To see how one school went about developing literacy strategies, examine the sample instructional plan in Figure 3.2. Are the state and local standards clearly addressed? Which of the literacy processes of reading, writing, speaking, listening, viewing, and thinking are used? What is the teacher planning to do before, during, and after reading to ensure that students achieve higher levels of engagement and learning? As you review your teachers' instructional plans, look for components similar to those outlined in this example.

The key is for your school to have an expectation that all teachers' instructional plans will be consistent with the standards and the achievement level of the students. Look again at Figure 3.2, which focuses on a middle school standard related to using reference materials. The teachers at this middle school, whether working in grade-level teams, vertical teams, or as individuals, are required to design instructional plans that address the use of reference materials. Their task is to provide enough structure and flexibility so that all students, regardless of their reading level and writing level, can meet the expectations. Given a choice of problems to research, discuss, write about, and present to their classmates, students will be using all of the literacy processes to address an important standard, thus improving reading and writing, as well as content knowledge. Instructional plans are written with high expectations for all students, incorporating literacy strategies to support student access to the content knowledge and skill in communicating what has been learned.

Let's pause for a moment to reflect on the reality of planning. There are a variety of approaches to instructional planning, each with its advantages.

❖ "Team planning" gives teachers the opportunity to share effective learning tools, teaching techniques, and assessment strategies. It also provides the perfect way for stronger teachers to support or coach weaker or novice teachers and for novice teachers to infuse new ideas and views while also building credibility with more senior staff.

❖ "Horizontal planning," a term used to describe planning conducted in grade-level teams, improves the consistency in students' learning expectations and experiences for that grade level. Using similar instructional plans, expectations, and grading strategies throughout a grade level can also eliminate, or at least reduce, the potential for parental complaints. Variations in expectations can

EXAMPLE

FIGURE 3.2
An 8th Grade Instructional Plan

State Strand: Reading, Listening, and Speaking as Processes

State Standards:

❖ A reader uses the reading process effectively.
❖ A reader constructs meaning from a wide range of texts.
❖ A listener uses effective listening strategies.
❖ A speaker uses effective speaking strategies.

8th Grade Benchmarks:

❖ Determines the essential message in text and identifies relevant details, facts, and patterns; identifies author's point of view; uses information to form inferences.
❖ Activates prior knowledge to predict content, purpose, and organization of selection and speaks for various purposes, audiences, and occasions.

Materials:

Copies of *Visions*, edited by Don Gallo, or *On the Bridge* by Todd Strasser; *Great Moves* by Sandy Asher; *A Hundred Bucks of Happy* by Susan Beth Pfeffer; and *Jeremiah's Song* by Walter Dean Myers.

Instructional Strategy

Before reading:
1. As a class, brainstorm some important choices that teenagers have to make. List these on the board.
2. Students will answer the following question in their writing journal: What is an important choice that you have had to make in your life? What did you decide to do? If you could make this decision over again, what would you do differently?
3. Students will write and share journal entries.

Reprinted by permission of Orange County (Fla.) Public Schools from the *Orange County 1997 Middle School Language Arts Core Curriculum Guide*.

EXAMPLE

FIGURE 3.2
(continued)

During reading:

4. Divide students into literature circles of 4–5 students.
5. Each group will receive copies of one story that they will read.
6. Tell the group that at the end of the reading time, the group will present the following information to the class. Students should look over *a* to *e* and, as a group, clarify what they are looking for before they begin reading. While reading, they may note their answers.

   a. Ask one student to summarize the story and report out.
   b. Ask each group to decide what the choice or decision was within the story. One person will explain the choice.
   c. Ask each group to decide if the decision the character(s) made was a good one. Why or why not? One person from each group will explain the group's decision.
   d. Ask each group: Did the character take the road less traveled? One person from each group will share this answer.
   e. Ask each group: Do you know of anyone real or fictional who has faced problems like these? What did they do? One person from each group will share this answer.

After reading:

7. Students will comment orally or in their academic logs about what was learned from this activity. Questions might include the following: How will you use what was learned in your own life? Which of the stories seems most interesting? (The class might benefit from a mini-lesson on reflection prior to this activity.)

8. Extension activities include

   ❖ Find examples of real-life situations where a person made a difficult choice. Did the person take the easy path or the difficult one? (Student could collect these in a class scrapbook.)
   ❖ Draw a map of the paths a person might choose. (Students might make chapter titles of major life events similar to road signs along the path.)
   ❖ Find other samples of literature that reflect this theme, such as Robert Frost's "The Road Not Taken" or Shel Silverstein's "Decisions." (Students might create a project that demonstrates their understanding of the literature.)
   ❖ Read *The Giver* by Lois Lowry. Explain Jonas's experience with "The Road to Elsewhere."

create perceptions of favoritism; consistency often makes it easier for parents to be supportive.

❖ "Vertical planning," in which teachers from multiple grade levels focus on the same standard, ensures that the level of difficulty in students' expectations is appropriately graduated and that the grading is consistent and meaningful. Vertical planning should result in measurable growth in students' skill and knowledge in a given strand as they move through the grades.

When working with teams of teachers to redesign our district's curriculum grade level by grade level, we found that using horizontal and vertical planning teams was the perfect way to cross-check the quality of our work and the level of difficulty we set for students' performance expectations. Interestingly, we found that the language arts curriculum expectations set for 5th graders were higher than those for 6th graders. This finding led us to make significant modifications to both the 5th and 6th grade levels of the language arts curriculum. (Take another look at Figure 3.2 for an excellent example of an 8th grade instructional plan that shows the relationship between standards, curriculum, and instructional strategies.)

As we worked on aligning the curriculum system, teachers continued to bring up the instructional strategy of integrated and interdisciplinary units. They felt that instituting standards by content area was philosophically in conflict with what they had learned about the importance of helping students make connections between learning experiences. Even though curriculum standards are usually developed and aligned within content areas, it's still a desirable strategy for teachers from different content areas to plan integrated and interdisciplinary units. For students to improve their reading and writing, all teachers in the school must understand and implement appropriate literacy strategies. After the curriculum is aligned horizontally (across a single grade level) and vertically (from grade to grade), the next enhancement is for grade-level interdisciplinary teams to develop units to support student learning. This interdisciplinary planning is more difficult to do at the high school level than it is in middle school, but it's a challenge worth undertaking. The result is the application of literacy process-related standards and benchmarks—things all students need to be successful—in all content areas. The payoff in student learning is great.

Question 3: Do both classroom and standardized assessments reflect actual classroom practice?

There is so much pressure today for accountability in the schools that some educators immediately get defensive when they hear the word "assessment." And there's no denying that most educators—teachers and administrators alike—have long resented how much time standardized assessment seems to take away from teaching time. Generally speaking, when we're with students we're most interested in the teaching and less interested in the assessing. We would like to show you how taking the classroom and standardized assessments one step further can complete a curriculum system focused on literacy.

Several years ago, as part of a curriculum alignment project, we conducted teacher workshops on assessment. So many teachers wanted to attend that we had to add additional sessions and keep waiting lists. You may be wondering why, if the topic of assessment does not generate much excitement from teachers, these workshops were in such great demand. The answer is that these teachers realized that aligning both classroom assessments and standardized assessments with their instruction made their instruction stronger. We opened each workshop by explaining to the participants that by improving classroom assessments, they could improve their students' learning. "Assessment is your friend," we told them, and although our participants chuckled some at the phrase, the message stuck. Teachers who understand assessment can use this knowledge to become more effective teachers. Soon they understand that when they design their assessment first, they are able to design clearer instructional plans to help students develop the knowledge and understanding the assessments will measure. This alignment between practice and assessment improves test scores and student learning.

The third of our list of critical questions for developing an aligned curriculum system asks you to explore how well your school's classroom instruction aligns with both standardized assessments and classroom assessments.

Aligning standardized assessment with classroom instruction. Start by identifying all the grade-level standards that will be assessed on the standardized test. These should be included in your school curriculum and should be among the essential learnings that you expect all students to know and be able to do. Again, this doesn't mean every standard and benchmark you believe to be essential will be on the big test; many things that are very important for students to learn do not lend themselves to standardized assessment.

Next, determine how teachers plan to assess the standards and benchmarks in the classroom. We recommend that teachers' instruction and classroom assessments use the same vocabulary, phrasing, and indicators of performance used in the official standards document, which will be the basis for the high-stakes assessment. If the assessment is not based on the standards, but has been selected for accountability purposes, then teachers' classroom instruction should incorporate the study materials, parent materials, and test preparation materials produced by the test publisher to ensure consistency in vocabulary, language, and style. It is also valuable to address the standards and benchmarks in the classroom in the same way they will be addressed on the high-stakes assessment. For example, if 60 percent of reading selections on the assessment are nonfiction, then 60 percent of classroom reading selections should be nonfiction so that students have adequate preparation. Likewise, students need plenty of in-class practice with the assessment's response format, whether it's bubble sheets, short answers, or writing prompts.

When teachers teach the measured standards and benchmarks is equally critical. A few years ago, our district was analyzing our students' scores on a particular high-stakes test and trying to figure out how to improve them. We were surprised to discover that many teachers were teaching some of the more difficult benchmarks *after* the testing date. No wonder our students were scoring low on certain items! Your teachers might use a format like the Essential Learnings Calendar template in Figure 3.3 to track what the essential learnings are and when they should be taught to and mastered by students.

To wrap up, there are four key points to keep in mind when aligning your curriculum and standardized assessment:

❖ Identify essential learnings for each grade level both within and beyond the official curriculum.
❖ Identify effective literacy strategies for your students.
❖ Identify measured standards for each grade level.
❖ Identify when students are learning the measured standards.

TEMPLATE

FIGURE 3.3
Essential Learnings Calendar

Measured Essential Learnings	Dates Taught or Mastered

Aligning classroom assessment with classroom instruction. Teachers should develop their classroom assessments at the same time they develop their instructional plans. As we know, a basic instructional plan will include what information or skills we want students to learn, what activities or assignments the students will do to learn the information or skills, and how we will know whether or not each student has learned the targeted information or skills. The work students produce during the activities should be the assessment.

During the instructional plan development and the development of the assessment, teachers also need to decide the criteria they will use to grade the assessment. The performance standard, the criteria for the activity or assignment, and the value assigned to the parts of the activity or assignment compose the grading system or rubric. Think back to the example of the assignment on using reference tools, in Figure 3.2 (see page 46). For this assignment, the teacher would have provided the students with a rubric for grading at the time the assignment was given. The rubric would have outlined what the students were expected to do in the reference tool assignment, how much each part of the assignment was worth, and the point system to be used to arrive at a grade. A separate rubric would be designed for the presentation on oral communication— a precursor to reading and writing. Telling students what is expected of them for the whole instructional experience will help them to understand the relationship of each part of the unit to the whole unit and also help them reach the teachers' expectations. It is hard enough for struggling students to feel motivated without having them try to guess what is important in a given assignment. Consistent use of the same rubric throughout the year will increase the success level of students. Remember: Assessment is your friend! More importantly, it's your students' friend as well.

Question 4: Do the learning tools in your school support the curriculum, instructional strategies, and assessments?

Learning tools are the resources teachers use to help students master the essential learnings in the curriculum. Grade-level textbooks are usually the first examples that come to mind. Others include software, Internet access, library/media resources, classroom libraries, technological hardware, and cameras. In Chapter 4, we address learning tools in greater depth, but here we want to discuss learning tools as they relate to curriculum system alignment.

It's a fairly obvious statement, but because of its critical importance we will go ahead and say it: The core resources your students use (usually textbooks) should focus on the essential learnings teachers identify for each grade level. If there are any essential learnings (within the official curriculum and measured standards or otherwise) that your core resources do *not* address in sufficient quantity and quality, you will need to supplement those core resources with carefully selected trade books, software, or teacher-made resources that do address them. For consistency, we recommend that major selections of learning tools be made in consultation with your Literacy Leadership Team.

After you have made sure that the learning tools available to teachers are aligned with the essential learnings, you must ensure that the instructional strategies the core and supplementary materials advocate are consistent with the strategies you have determined to be best for your students. As a positive example, perhaps the publisher of your U.S. History textbook includes a class set of Karen Hesse's *Out of the Dust*, complete with discussion questions and related activities, to supplement the textbook's coverage of the Dust Bowl Era. Shared reading of *Out of the Dust*, perhaps using audiotapes, and shared quick-writes would provide consistency in curriculum, learning tools, and instructional strategies. As a negative example, perhaps the publisher of your U.S. History text does not provide (or even reference) any trade books to supplement its coverage of the Dust Bowl Era or incorporate strategies in the teacher's edition beyond "read and summarize." If strategies are not explicit in the learning tools your teachers are using, ask the teachers to identify how they intend to incorporate effective instructional strategies using those materials.

The last phase in addressing alignment with the learning tools is to be sure that these tools include or address the measured standards. What's more, this inclusion should be explicit—not just hinted at or embedded—so it's easily recognizable to both students and teachers. For example, if your state measures a middle or high school standard requiring students to recognize cause-and-effect relationships in literary texts, this skill should be clearly addressed in the student materials. Otherwise, it may fall to teachers to determine when and how to teach it. When this happens, teaching directly to the standard is often omitted, resulting in lower student achievement. In addition, the techniques for assessment included in each learning tool should be in line philosophically with both the school's philosophy of what is important *and* should provide practice for standardized assessment. Assessments reflecting higher-order thinking, problem solving, and application will encourage teacher incorporation of literacy processes; assessments that focus mostly on basic recall will not. You may have to have both core and supplementary learning tools to find the balance that your staff has identified as appropriate.

By now, you are probably wondering if it's possible to align so extensively in a middle school, much less in a large high school! Yes, it *is* possible—and we assure you that it will jump-start gains in student achievement. Remember Dr. Paul Van Mitchell, the principal we introduced in Chapter 1? He's an example of a school leader who spearheaded this kind of alignment. In Van's high school of more than 3,000 students from diverse backgrounds, he and his teaching staff worked extensively to align the curriculum both across each grade level and from 9th through 12th grades. During the alignment process, Van and his teachers learned that there were some very important skills and content that they were not teaching (and in fact, had never taught) and that some content was repeated from grade to grade. They also learned that they had been basically teaching what was in their textbooks, which did not address many of the standards measured on their state assessments. Today, Van's faculty members are focused on what they have agreed to teach (rather than on individual preference of what they want to teach) and they use a variety of learning tools (not just textbooks) to ensure standards coverage. As a collaborative team, the faculty has joined together in their commitment to all students becoming joyful, independent readers and writers. Amazing as it may seem, five years ago, Van's school was ranked seventh out of 12 high schools in student achievement; today, it is ranked fifth of 14.

Question 5: How will you eliminate unproductive practice?

Congratulate yourself when you and your teachers have gotten this far in the alignment process. You will have achieved a major accomplishment as a fail-safe literacy leader. The next question to address, and the subsequent steps you must take to answer it, will be a challenge.

Teachers may not be resistant to the idea of alignment, because they are well aware of the need for accountability and higher student achievement. But you should expect many to be resistant when you ask, "Are there any unproductive practices in the school that we should eliminate because they are taking valuable learning time from our students?"

Why raise this question if it will create controversy and resistance? It's simple: In order to make time to target the new expectations you have just created, you must let go of something. Eliminating unproductive practices will allow you to regain and reallocate the precious resource of time.

What do you think the teachers will say should be eliminated? In our experience, before teachers focus on the classroom, they will usually target administrative practices. A warning, then: If you are not open to considering administrative issues for elimination, you would be better off not incorporating this step in your alignment process. Among administrative practices, likely targets include intercom interruptions, pep rallies, assemblies, testing, test preparation, scheduling problems, large class sizes, and insufficient budget for materials. When the focus does turn to instructional practices, those that principals and teachers frequently identify for elimination include busy work, in-class time for homework, free time, and outdated courses.

Every school will identify different items for this list. After you've compiled a list of potentially unproductive practices, you will need to design a plan for working toward eliminating the *most* unproductive ones—both administrative and instructional. (As a principal, it is a good idea to show your faculty that you are willing to make changes first, before you expect them to do so.) We recommend working with your Literacy Leadership Team to prioritize the items on your list, starting with the ones that the team perceives will be the easiest to cut. You and your team can then begin the brainstorming and problem solving necessary to do away with these unproductive practices.

Question 6: How will you know that your curriculum system is aligned?

Now that you have worked with your teachers to create an aligned curriculum system, you will need to periodically evaluate the progress you've made toward this goal. Continued use of a Curriculum System Alignment Chart (see Figure 3.1, page 41) will help you with this evaluation and enable you to identify which areas still need some attention. Finally, you will want to inform all teachers, parents, students, and the community about the new curriculum system you have developed and keep them abreast of system progress so they will understand the decisions you make about purchases, school events, and priorities.

In the Classroom

As the middle school principal, I walk through classes every day. Sometimes I linger and observe students, noting the level of engagement and the importance of the work being done. These observations help me to have reflective conversations with teachers about how to improve learning for all of our diverse student body.

This morning, I'm struck by the high level of engagement in an 8th grade language arts class that is full of students who can be exceptionally challenging both in and out of class. Joyce, the teacher, has expressed concerns to me about the various reading levels in the class and how well her students may achieve standards (particularly, how they will perform on our state reading and writing tests). She has filled her room with student work in all states of progress toward excellence. There are bookshelves overflowing with reading material, both fiction and nonfiction, on a variety of reading levels and topics of interest. I even see books on tape for the students who don't read on grade level.

Joyce opens the class today, as she has every day this week, by reading from Lois Lowry's *The Giver*. Before beginning the reading, she asks the students to "quick write" for one minute, predicting what they think will happen in today's chapter. I'm surprised that I don't hear the moaning ("Do we *have* to?" and "I don't want to write!") that I hear in some classes. Here, the writing happens so quickly that before I know it, the students have finished and are raising their hands to share their predictions. (Am I in a middle school classroom?) Joyce charts these predictions so that students can refer to them later.

After her students have accessed their prior knowledge and thought about what will happen next, Joyce jumps right into the chapter. The students follow along in their books as she reads with a high degree of expression, pausing to ask them to think or modeling a think-aloud just as an expert reader would. The students seem to love being read to and enjoy the age-appropriate selection. As I listen, I can understand why they were anxious to get started.

As the shared reading ends, Joyce instructs the students to write a one-sentence summary and an "I wonder." I ask a student named Lupe what she thinks about being read to and these short writing assignments. Lupe tells me that before these shared readings, she didn't know that books were so interesting. It makes her want to read more. They have read other texts this way: *The House on Mango Street* by Sandra Cisneros and *Out of the Dust* by Karen Hesse. As for the short writing, Lupe informs me that middle school students don't like to write a lot, but when they are asked to write only one sentence at a time every day, "Before you know it, you've written a lot."

Lupe tells me that when they read *The House on Mango Street*, they wrote daily, and at the end of the novel, they organized all the daily writings into longer pieces that made a lot of sense. This technique makes writing easier for students, at least according to Lupe. She adds that sometimes she draws a little to get the ideas flowing, and this doesn't bother her teacher at all! In fact, her teacher *encourages* her to draw and to share with her classmates how drawing helps her to understand the reading. Lupe says she bets that they'll have to write about how Jonas in *The Giver* relates to other characters, to themselves, and to the world—the teacher is s-o-o-o-o predictable!

I let Lupe get back to her summary sentence. Soon, Joyce is asking for volunteers to read their summary sentence to the rest of the class. Several students read, and Joyce charts each summary sentence next to the predictions they made earlier. I was listening for the "correct answer," but Joyce encourages and applauds the differences between the summaries, commenting that she can tell they are expert readers because they have each made their own meaning in connecting to the novel. Then, she asks them how their predictions compare with their summaries. I notice that some students are making notes while the discussion goes on. Joyce encourages them to add anything they hear that has meaning for them to their log of summaries.

As I leave the classroom, I reflect on the high level of participation, high level of thinking, and positive relationships in the classroom. A teacher like Joyce doesn't need to worry about standards and assessment. Her diverse students are working hard, with relevance and rigor. They are writing more every day than students of teachers who assign long essays and then get frustrated when students don't finish the work. Such alignment of standards, instruction, learning tools, and assessment will result in great growth for Joyce's students. I'm anxious to see it.

Review and reflection

Creating a fail-safe system of literacy has been a lot of work so far. Making the commitment to get started was easy. Carefully studying the data to determine what really needed to happen with your curriculum system took some time and support from outside of the school. Aligning the curriculum system was a time-consuming process that took some collaborative work, but now the teachers are on the same page and ready to teach what they have to, as well as what they want to, in ways that your students will learn best. The next chapter will lead you through a process for careful examination and creation of classrooms for literacy learning to give your teachers and students an edge. Your staff will enjoy it!

Further reading in alignment of curriculum, instruction, learning tools, and assessment

Carr, J. F., & Harris, D. E. (2001). *Succeeding with standards: Linking curriculum, assessment, and action planning.* Alexandria, VA: Association for Supervision and Curriculum Development.

Erickson, H. L. (1998). *Concept-based curriculum: Teaching beyond the facts.* Thousand Oaks, CA: Corwin Press.

Harris, D. E., & Carr, J. F. (1996). *How to use standards in the classroom.* Alexandria, VA: Association for Supervision and Curriculum Development.

Taylor, R. (1999, December). Missing pieces; aligned curriculum, instruction, and assessment. *Schools in the Middle, 9*(4), 14–16.

Taylor, R. (2002, September). Creating a system that gets results for older, reluctant readers. *Phi Delta Kappan, 84*(1), 85–87.

Wiggins, G., & McTighe, J. (1998). *Understanding by design.* Alexandria, VA: Association for Supervision and Curriculum Development.

4

Creating Classrooms for Literacy Learning

So FAR, WE HAVE FOCUSED ON FAIL-SAFE LITERACY LEADERSHIP THAT WILL LAY THE foundation for all students to become joyful, independent readers and writers. Creating the kind of classroom that enhances literacy learning requires new thinking about what the students should be doing daily and about how classrooms will look, sound, and feel. In this chapter, we ask you to lead your school to set expectations that will articulate exactly what teachers must do to support literacy learning in every classroom. These expectations will not limit teachers, but rather, will support wise instructional decisions on a daily basis, first by communicating to teachers what's expected of them, and second, by serving as criteria for determining which learning tools are needed to reach all learners. We provide the fail-safe point of view of what high-performing teachers do, and we believe that if your teachers do these things consistently, your students' achievement will soar.

The fail-safe literacy point of view

The fail-safe literacy point of view has three essential components, which together provide a comprehensive, balanced way to improve adolescent literacy:

1. Consistent incorporation of the literacy processes of reading, writing, listening, speaking, viewing, and thinking

2. Explicit teaching and incorporation of literacy strategies
3. Accountable independent reading every day

Let's examine each component in depth.

Component 1: Consistent incorporation of the literacy processes

We have defined literacy processes as reading, writing, speaking, listening, viewing, and thinking. Teachers will agree that students need to use these literacy processes in all classes to access content knowledge and to communicate what they have learned. What's more, these processes develop together and specifically support the development of reading comprehension and writing—the foundation for middle and high school students' success in all coursework and the focus of standardized assessment.

One of the most expedient ways to improve students' reading and writing (and thus, improve their content learning), is to set the expectation that all teachers deliberately use each of these literacy processes in their instruction. This will mean that regardless of the content to be taught, teachers will support students in reading, writing about their reading, and speaking about their reading, as well as analyzing and thinking about their reading. In addition, viewing (through technology and other means) requires thinking and analysis, which students should then discuss and write about. As simple as this seems, if all of your teachers commit to purposefully, deliberately, and regularly incorporating all of the processes of literacy, you will see vocabulary, comprehension, and writing improve across content areas. Content teachers will find that their students' understanding and communication of learning in their classes will also improve.

Component 2: Explicit teaching and incorporation of literacy strategies

Although we know that content teachers expect students to read and respond to their on-grade-level* textbooks independently, at least half of the middle and high school students in the United States cannot read well enough to do so. The 1998 National Assessment of Educational Progress (NAEP) report card states that 40 percent of 4th graders and 25 percent

*Statistically, "on-grade-level" is defined as in the 50th percentile.

of 8th and 12th graders read below the basic level (Donahue, Voelkl, Campbell, & Mazzeo, 1999, p. 2).

Expert readers approach text strategically, predicting, summarizing, questioning, clarifying, visualizing, and making connections. Therefore, the way to help all students become expert readers and content learners is to explicitly teach them the literacy strategies of expert readers:

❖ *Before-reading strategies* help readers to access prior knowledge and develop vocabulary and complex, content-related concepts so that new learning can take place. Examples include analyzing the book jacket, looking at illustrations and making predications about the content, and brainstorming what is already known about the content to be learned.

❖ *During-reading strategies,* like prediction, concept organizers, and one-sentence summaries, help readers make personal connections with the text, clarifying and deepening emerging understandings of what they are reading.

❖ *After-reading strategies,* such as developing story maps or sequence charts, developing factual and inferential questions, and writing about how before-reading predictions differed from the actual outcomes, help readers to analyze, summarize, and connect the current reading to other texts, other concepts, and the world outside of school.

The responsibility for explicitly teaching these strategies should fall to your reading, language arts, or English teachers. They should also commit to using these strategies in their classrooms before reading assignments, during reading, and after reading to build students' competence and confidence. Together, these literacy strategies will assist all students in accessing and deepening understanding of content learning.

Component 3: Accountable independent reading every day

Using literacy processes in all classes enhances students' vocabulary and content knowledge. Incorporation of literacy strategies builds their vocabulary, concept development, and comprehension. These two components prepare students for the third in our fail-safe approach: the daily accountable independent reading that helps them to build fluency and comprehension, both of which are necessary to improve overall reading.

While students should read in every class, accountable independent reading is something distinct: it is self-paced, in-class reading (at least 20 minutes each day) of selections that match a student's independent reading level and individual interests. Each student is held accountable for what he or she reads in whatever manner the teacher deems appropriate—for example, through reading logs, daily follow-up questions, and short summaries.

Daily accountable independent reading is not usually expected in middle and high schools. If it is, it's usually limited to reading intervention classrooms. Based on our experience, we firmly believe that it should be a feature of *all* schools and for *all* students, with responsibility assigned to specific teachers (usually reading, language arts, or English teachers). Accountable independent reading gives students the time they need to apply and strengthen their evolving literacy skills. It allows them to practice reading strategies they have been taught and to make personal connections with reading materials they have chosen.

We have seen firsthand how accountable independent reading enhances students' joy in reading and writing. Older, struggling students—students who haven't experienced reading as joyful and are unaware that it can be—are particular beneficiaries. The enjoyment they experience motivates continued reading, developing the literacy and comprehension that raises reading scores.

In sum, for students to maximize their literacy development and content learning, they must apply literacy processes, use the strategies of expert readers, and read independently with accountability, all on a daily basis. Improvement takes practice, and it's no different with literacy. Schools that use some but not all of the fail-safe literacy system components we outline will have results that fall short of expectations; it takes all three to develop joyful, independent readers and writers capable of meeting the literacy requirements of middle and high school coursework.

Creating an environment for literacy learning

Creating an environment in middle and high schools where literacy flourishes means making classrooms physically, academically, and psychologically safe for learning. Students must believe that they are significant members of a community of learners—all of whom have important work to do, all of whom can succeed on that work, and all of whom will receive respect and encouragement as they strive for success. When students trust their teacher and their classmates, even the weaker students will take risks to read, write, ask questions, and participate.

When this feeling of community is absent, students are afraid to try. Here's a comment we've encountered again and again from struggling students: "If I think the teacher is going to call on me, I'll put my head down and say I'm sick to avoid reading." Other students tell us how they resort to more drastic coping methods: "Sometimes, I just reach over and punch someone or act bad so the teacher will throw me out."

Building the trust of your community of learners pays off in more and better student engagement, less misbehavior, and higher student achievement. To create this kind of environment, teachers must incorporate instruction they can adapt to meet the literacy needs of each student with positive literacy experiences, strategy lessons, and accountable independent reading. The more confident and successful each student feels, the more risks to learn each will take. In the subsections that follow, we discuss our view of the ideal environment for fail-safe literacy learning in terms of organization, grouping, learning experiences, and learning tools. We address reading/language arts/English classrooms separately from other content area classrooms because the reading/language arts/English classroom is the model for literacy learning and the place where the majority of literacy learning is concentrated. However, we believe it's essential that all classrooms incorporate literacy processes and literacy strategies before, during, and after reading to deepen comprehension of content text and expand literacy learning.

Expectations for the literacy-focused reading/language arts/ English classroom

To reach a diversity of students, teachers should use a variety of methods and commensurate learning tools each day and each week. In providing our example of an expectation of the good literacy-focused language arts/reading classroom and its commensurate learning tools, we are incorporating three kinds of instructional organization: whole-class instruction, small-group work, and learning stations or centers that are focused on accountable independent reading and writing. You will notice that each grouping uses technology and media strategically and deliberately to enhance reading and writing.

Some of the approaches we recommend, particularly flexible grouping and the use of learning centers or stations, are rather unusual in middle and high schools. This is unfortunate, as these are among the easiest and most effective ways to reach all students. Many teachers accustomed to traditional, whole-class instruction aren't readily prepared to incorporate these strategies in their classrooms and will require professional development to learn how to implement them (see Chapter 5).

Now, let's take a closer look at what a teacher might do during the various approaches and with the kinds of learning tools these approaches require.

Whole-class instruction. During whole-class instruction, teachers may teach in a traditional way by providing direct instruction related to the curriculum standards. Our literacy-focused expectations for whole-class instruction in reading/language arts/English classrooms include that teachers model the use of reading and writing strategies (see Component 1, page 60) and explain spelling, usage, and the mechanics of grammar.

To this, we would add an expectation to incorporate read-alouds (when only the teacher reads) and shared reading (when the teacher reads and students follow along in their books). These two approaches bring the joy of reading to life, giving all students—from the poorest reader to the most advanced—access to required texts above their independent reading level and to genres with which they might not be familiar. They model for students what expert readers do and provide opportunities for teaching vocabulary, grammar, punctuation, and phonics in context. Not only do these strategies provide access to content knowledge in language arts, they are vital in helping students experience academic safety. Enhanced ability to access important information lowers student frustration levels, resulting in fewer classroom discipline issues and higher student achievement.

Rose: *When working with teachers and administrators from middle and high schools, questions always arise about whether or not the students value read-alouds and shared reading. Without fail, teachers and administrators* *will voice support for these activities, commenting on how positively students respond to them and how student achievement goes up as a result. This happens because the teachers select developmentally appropriate picture books, nonfiction, or adolescent literature that is strategically connected to the standards-based curriculum they are teaching. The read-alouds and shared reading teach vocabulary and concepts, while motivating students to learn more before they scaffold into the textbooks where the same content may not be presented in so engaging a format. Nancy, a longtime colleague and literacy specialist, is in the habit of asking her former students (now adults) for their fondest memories of her junior high class. Consistently, each former student will recall Nancy's reading to them and note how connected it made them feel to her, to the other students, and to what they were learning.*

Valerie: *During a recent monthly high school visit, I asked teachers to share any "ahas" or successes they'd experienced early on in their language arts or reading classrooms. One after the other, they all expressed amazement at their high school students' positive reactions to read-alouds. Their immediate connection was that it allowed every student an opportunity to hear, understand, and learn from the text without feeling threatened. Furthermore, it clarified for the teachers the limitations of round robin reading (a staple of many secondary classrooms), where students take turns reading out loud when it's their turn, regardless of their reading ability. In contrast, read-alouds eliminated undue pressure and created an enhanced level of trust among teachers and students.*

What should you look for in learning tools that will support literacy-focused whole-class instruction? In most middle and high school English and language arts programs, the major learning tool is the anthology of literature, which incorporates various genres. Because anthologies are expensive and tend to be used for up to 10 years, be sure to select them on the basis of objective criteria. Here are some guidelines:

❖ *Look for alignment with your curriculum standards.* For example, the ratio of fiction to nonfiction within an anthology should reflect what you'll find on local, state, and national assessments, which do emphasize nonfiction over fiction. If your anthologies omit nonfiction selections, you'll want to provide teachers and students with appropriate supplementary texts to support your language arts and content curriculum standards. (Of course, when reading, language arts, and English teachers incorporate a large proportion of nonfiction, they will be supporting the students in their content classes of science, social studies, and mathematics, as well as in their reading and writing assessments.)

❖ *Look for compatibility with your range of reading levels.* Be sure that the students who will be using a text can read that text. As you're likely to have quite a wide range of reading levels in your school (clarified through data gathering and analysis), you may want to select one anthology for above-average readers and another for students reading below their grade level. For students with the lowest reading level (those with reading scores that fall in stanines 1–2), anthologies will probably not be very useful, as these students need an intensive intervention program designed for their unique learning needs; however, this program should be built on the same classroom expectations set for other learners.

❖ *Look for compatibility with student profiles.* Traditional anthologies, which tend to be thick and heavy with small print and few visual components to create interest or indicate connections to adolescents' own lives, are very often intimidating and uninviting to the older reader. When choosing an anthology, keep readability in mind. Also, the pieces included should be respectful of the students—that is, they should reflect a diversity of language, ethnicity, and cultural backgrounds so that students can identify with the characters, plots, settings, and authors. This is critical in supporting students' motivation to read and to complete their assignments.

❖ *Look for compatibility with preferred instructional and literacy strategies.* In terms of the teacher support included in the anthology, look for sample assignments that are consistent with the instructional strategies you believe are effective and consistent with the alignment of your curriculum and instruction. For instance, if you are supportive of graphic organizers, look for them in the teacher materials. Some teacher materials will even organize sample lessons with before-reading, during-reading, and after-reading activities. Also, seek out materials that support English language learners and students with learning disabilities. Finally, the teacher materials selected should assist the teacher in integrating reading, writing, grammar, and spelling.

❖ *Look for applicability to the world outside the classroom.* It's especially important that teaching materials for middle and high school students be relevant to them in terms of content and application to the real world. Higher-level applications and research using technology should appear in each unit of study. Most publishers offer Web sites that provide supplementary support for contemporary topics, authors, and events.

In addition to anthologies, middle and high school teachers need carefully selected class sets of young adult, contemporary, and classic literature for shared reading. Thematic pairing of young adult literature with classic literature is a great way to motivate students to do their best work. Video adaptations of books and stories are another good option, provided that students watch these as a pre-reading comprehension strategy rather than as an end-of-unit reward. Videos can be an effective way to introduce setting, characters, historical context, and plot—especially for older reluctant readers, who may have difficulty creating mental representations of the people and events they encounter in printed texts. In fact, providing videos as a scaffold to reading printed text enhances comprehension for both reluctant *and* skilled readers.

Small-group instruction. Our ideal reading/language arts/English classroom will also incorporate daily small-group instruction to ensure that all learners have maximized opportunities for learning. Small-group instruction may sound like an unusual expectation for a good secondary language arts or reading teacher, but the flexibility it provides makes it a particularly effective way to meet the differing needs of students within a single classroom. In general, small-group work allows teachers to bring together students with similar needs and give them attention tailored to those needs—whether that be additional challenge for the very advanced students or focused, skill-building instruction for the less advanced. It can also be a time to coach and direct cooperative groups working on special projects. A teacher might also provide direct instruction to one or more groups of students, coach other groups in certain strategies, or meet in private conferences with individuals. While the groups read and discuss their findings, the teacher might support the literacy development of other students through guided reading and guided writing strategies.

Students enjoy small-group instruction not only because of the academic success these groups help them to experience, but also because of the opportunities it affords for more personalized attention from their teachers. Secondary students, unlike elementary school students, are less likely to have such personal academic time with a caring adult.

Learning tools for small-group work may be the same as what's used in the whole group (the anthology, class sets of carefully selected literature) or may be fully differentiated supplementary materials (for example, particular texts selected for different levels of reading proficiency). When students are grouped based on their independent reading level, those who are reading the same book might support each other in understanding and writing about it. Other teachers might ask students within a small group to each read a different book on the same theme and then share what they are reading and writing about it. This technique is motivating because it permits students to select reading material they're interested in and explore it without the sense that they are "competing" with their peers to understand it. It also exposes students to a broader array of texts; after the small group work is complete, some may be inspired to read the selections of their group members.

Learning tools that may be particularly useful for small-group instruction in reading/language arts/English classrooms are teacher's edition anthologies that include skill-building activities, graphic organizers, writing prompts, and comprehension strategies. Also needed are young adult literature and nonfiction titles representing a range of reading levels in sets of six to eight. Supplementary skill development kits may also have a place. These kits are fairly inexpensive and can be effective in motivating students to work on skill-building and comprehension strategies during small-group instruction.

Learning centers and stations. Learning centers and stations allow teachers to maximize both time and resources. What's more, they are very effective ways to differentiate instruction based on varying readiness levels and interests of adolescents, providing interest-based motivation for students to engage in the work. Learning centers and stations also support students' developmental needs to have physical movement, different choices, and changes of learning activities. We recommend setting up stations that focus on small-group work, on technology, on writing (an "Author's Corner"), and on accountable independent reading.

The last two—reading centers and writing centers—are the most critical for literacy-focused classrooms. As we've stressed, daily accountable independent reading is one of three essential components of a fail-safe literacy system because it ensures the practice necessary to build reading fluency and because the personal choice involved makes the reading interesting and meaningful. Even the highly skilled readers we speak with often comment that before accountable independent reading became a regular feature in their classrooms, their reading assignments never included anything that *they* enjoyed—just what the teacher liked. For the developing reader, daily accountable independent reading can be transformational, often allowing them to experience joy in reading for the very first time. Also, when students are interested in a topic or have learned that they like a particular author, they will often read more difficult pieces, stretching themselves to higher levels of comprehension and vocabulary. For these reasons, we regard accountable independent reading as essential work for both the good reader and the reluctant one.

Please note that we have purposefully identified it as *accountable* independent reading; accountability systems such as reading logs and end-of-reading projects are very much a part of the plan. And also note that teachers who decide to use quizzes to monitor progress in reading comprehension must determine in advance what level of quiz performance is required before a student will be permitted to move on to the next selection. If the student does not perform satisfactorily on the quiz, the teacher must decide what steps to take next with the student. Also, remember that successful use of accountable independent reading stations requires that the student make the choice of what to read. Choosing a book to read (with the guidance of a teacher) helps to motivate students. If they find that a book is too difficult or boring, they must be permitted to choose another book, as long as it falls within reasonable parameters determined by the teacher and students.

Motivating adolescents to read independently requires a large and varied classroom library with a ratio of 15–20 books for each student. When we point this out to faculties in the schools we work with, many respond that they have a wonderful selection of books in the central library. The question we ask them (and that you must ask yourself) is, "Do all students regularly engage in independent reading with those books, or would it be easier for both the student and teacher to have these resources within the classroom?" In our opinion, if a school sets the expectation that classroom teachers will use accountable independent reading every day, then the resources necessary to do this need to be within the classroom.

The print materials in classroom libraries should represent a variety of reading levels, interest areas, and genres. Selections should also represent a variety of cultures, language backgrounds, and ethnicities. Any young adult literature included should be selected by the teacher, media specialist, or someone who knows the students. Although this kind of literature is often engaging to adolescents, the subject matter can be sensitive. (Be sure that young adult selections are previewed by someone who knows the school community very well.) Along with young adult literature, the independent reading area should be filled with magazines, manuals, informational texts, children's books, and classics. Supplementary reading comprehension kits on a variety of themes may also be included if teachers deem them necessary as a way to support the reluctant readers. Or a teacher may want to set up another station for specific skill development activities and rotate selections for these readers.

When stocking classroom libraries, also be sure to include audiobooks and CD-ROMs, which are excellent media to help reluctant readers become independent readers. Audiobooks provide access to on-grade level or above-grade level literature and content for students whose independent reading level is lower than the mean. CD-ROMs provide the same sort of scaffolding and may include video and graphics to help struggling readers create mental models of what's going on in the text. This kind of visualization, which enhances comprehension, vocabulary, and concept development, is routine for good readers, but rare for poor ones. Most publishers now provide these kinds of cross-media resources—online or as CDs—as companions to anthologies. Using such technological support for independent reading can motivate, support, and accelerate the literacy development of older, reluctant readers until they become confident, joyful, independent readers.

Having addressed reading centers, we must now turn to writing centers, which are essential in literacy-focused reading/language arts/English classrooms. Students should write daily about what they read and use vocabulary they have learned from their reading in what they write. The writing center may be just a table in the corner or center of the room with a sign above it reading "Author's Corner" or "Create and Connect." Materials that promote creative expression and make writing fun (e.g., markers, colored or bordered paper, colored pens and pencils, and a stapler) should be available. Copies of classroom rubrics used to assess writing and samples of "good" writing to use as models provide academic safety and support the students in successfully meeting the teacher's expectations. Resource materials such as dictionaries and grammar resources should also be available.

Many writing areas also feature computers. Giving students classroom access to software and the Internet can enhance their research, writing, and reading. Computers can also help them to develop multimedia presentations for demonstrating literacy development and content learning through creative, authentic products that incorporate video, music, graphics, and text. Many students who are challenged by reading and writing assignments flourish when they have opportunities to apply their skill or interest in technology, music, art, or dance to show what they have learned through their reading and writing. What's more, students observing the multimedia presentation are also practicing literacy (listening, viewing, thinking) and enhancing their vocabulary and concept knowledge.

Expectations for the literacy-focused content area classroom

Where in your school does the most difficult vocabulary, problem solving, and higher-order thinking take place? Is it in language arts and reading classes, or is it in science and social studies classes? Students generally have had less experience with the vocabulary, concepts, and subject matter of content classes and as a result, often find the reading work required there particularly difficult.

When we were evaluating the results of a middle school literacy intervention program, we were delighted to find that as students' reading comprehension skills improved, so did their grades in science, social studies, and mathematics. You also can expect your students' content reading and writing to get better with improvement in language arts and reading. But this improvement will occur only when your content classes purposefully and strategically incorporate good practice for comprehending printed text. For this reason, in addition to developing expectations for the good reading/language arts/English classroom and commensurate learning tools at your school, you'll want to consider developing parallel expectations and learning tools for the content classes. While content teachers may incorporate excellent strategies based on their curriculum, they may not always focus on how to help students comprehend printed text more easily.

Two of the easiest expectations to set are for content teachers to incorporate the processes of literacy (reading, writing, speaking, listening, viewing, and thinking) into their classroom instruction and to use literacy strategies. For example, before asking students to read a textbook chapter on weather systems, an earth science teacher might use a KNL (Know, Need to Know, Learned) organizer strategy, using diagrams, words, and pictures to activate students' prior knowledge about the topic, stimulate interest, and provide a clear purpose for reading—including what they expect to learn from the chapter. What's more, this strategy gives the teacher a frame of reference regarding where to focus instruction. During reading, the teacher might use prediction models, concept models, questioning techniques, or two-column note taking. After reading, the teacher might have students use graphic organizers (concept maps, webbing, sequence charts, cause and effect diagrams, another KNL organizer) to analyze information and draw conclusions or apply the concepts to their world. So much of what is covered in content area textbooks is abstract; literacy strategies used before, during, and after reading can help students represent content, concepts, and skills more concretely for deeper understanding and transference to long-term memory.

The main learning tool in content classes is, of course, the textbook, and many of the guidelines for selecting language arts anthologies apply here as well. Most obviously, a textbook written at a reading level higher than a student's independent reading level can present a formidable barrier to understanding. In these instances, the content teacher's use of literacy comprehension strategies is especially critical, as it can help students use prior knowledge and real-world experiences to bridge the gap and meet content standards. When struggling readers can connect the classroom to their real lives, their engagement and achievement improves. And, as with language arts anthologies, content texts should also be audited for alignment, ensuring that curriculum content standards are covered. Schools can further support reading and writing in the content areas by providing supplementary materials such as fiction and nonfiction selections related to content standards. This kind of coordination between the language arts teachers and content teachers can help students to see patterns in how instruction is delivered and to make connections between the knowledge they gain in language arts and the knowledge they gain in content area classes.

Steps for creating expectations for classrooms for literacy learning and selecting learning tools

So far in this chapter, we've presented guiding principles for creating expectations of literacy learning and selecting learning tools and discussed some examples of what these might look like. Now it's time for you to take the action yourself and lead your school to set expectations of its own. Here are the steps we recommend:

1. Create a Literacy Leadership Team (if you've not already done so).
2. Review the student data gathered and analyzed (see Chapter 2).
3. Research proven and promising literacy practices.
4. Set literacy expectations appropriate for your student population.
5. Align literacy expectations with learning tools appropriate for your student population.

Step 1: Create a Literacy Leadership Team

Establishing a Literacy Leadership Team is one of the most deliberate and strategic decisions that a literacy leader can make. If you have not already set up this team, do it now. We recommend that your Literacy Leadership Team represent all professional constituencies in the school, including each department, grade level, and the media center. The team's charge? Gather and review student data to determine priorities for literacy learning, as discussed in Chapter 2, and research proven and promising practices to set the expectation for the literacy classroom and support alignment of learning tools.

Step 2: Review the student data gathered and analyzed

If you've been following along with our recommendations, during your reading of Chapter 2, you (and perhaps your Literacy Leadership Team) launched an in-depth study of your students' achievement data. We mention it here because it is imperative to maintain the mental model of the students when creating classroom expectations and selecting learning tools. Yes, classroom expectations should reflect the standards-based curriculum, but they also should reflect the students in terms of their interests, diversity, and culture. You and your Literacy Leadership Team must keep these factors in mind when reviewing research and identifying components of the expectations for the literacy classroom.

Step 3: Research proven and promising literacy practices

As the literacy leader, you're responsible for working with your Literacy Leadership Team to study current research on adolescent reading, writing, and content learning. After reviewing the student data, the Literacy Leadership Team should focus on becoming knowledgeable about the most current proven and promising practices related to teaching adolescents and to literacy. A deep understanding of these research-based practices should guide the Literacy Leadership Team's design of your school's expectations for the literacy classroom. By strategically learning together, sharing what they find on Web sites, reading (the selections at the end of this chapter are a good place to start), and attending conferences and workshops, members of your Literacy Leadership Team will add value to their recommendations. They probably will find ideas and caveats to share with the entire faculty, along with recommendations regarding professional development.

According to Judith Langer, director of The National Research Center on English Language & Learning, the secondary school teachers who make the most difference in students' literacy learning use three key strategies: direct instruction, student practice, and integration. Teachers who use only two of the three strategies do not have the same positive results (Langer, 2000). *Direct instruction* is necessary to provide modeling and teach the literacy strategies that good readers and writers use before, during, and after reading. *Student practice* is imperative because it's through reading and writing that students make improvements in these vital literacy processes. *Integration* is the application of learning to the real world and the way that students derive meaning from the material they read and write. The hypothetical example of expectations for a fail-safe literacy classroom presented in the first half of this chapter incorporates this research.

The fail-safe literacy point of view we advocate synthesizes the research on adolescent literacy into three components. Here they are again:

1. Consistent incorporation of the literacy processes of reading, writing, listening, speaking, viewing, and thinking
2. Explicit teaching and incorporation of literacy strategies
3. Accountable independent reading every day

We believe that Literacy Leadership Teams that create expectations focused on these three components will accelerate all students' literacy learning and thus improve all students' access to standards-based curriculum. We're confident that the research you and your Team conduct will bring you to the same conclusion.

Step 4: Set literacy expectations appropriate for your student population

You and your Literacy Leadership team have analyzed your student population's literacy status, strengths, and weaknesses, paying particular attention to the needs of all student subgroups. You have done your research. Now, you and your team are ready to set specific expectations for what constitutes your ideal literacy-focused classroom, both in reading/English/language arts and in all content areas. You may wish to read this chapter's "In the Classroom" vignette, beginning on page 80, before doing so.

After the expectations are set, you and your team must set about the work of building faculty consensus for implementation. In our experience, the process of obtaining teacher-buy in motivates teachers to try new strategies and consider transformations in the classroom that will positively affect adolescents. After your staff reach a consensus on literacy learning expectations, they will support you in many ways on your quest to help all students become joyful, independent readers and writers.

Step 5: Align literacy expectations with learning tools appropriate for your student population

In middle and high schools, creating a classroom for literacy is putting in place a system where the learning expectations and teacher expectations are supported by learning tools consistent with the research about how adolescents are motivated, how teachers can best improve students' literacy processes and content knowledge, and how teachers can best address students' developmental needs. For this very practical reason, it is imperative that learning tools in the classroom are aligned with the curriculum, support the instructional strategies that you and your Literacy Leadership Team believe accelerate learning, and lead to success for your unique student population.

To ensure this alignment, the Literacy Leadership Team may try using a guide like Figure 4.1's Effective Learning Tools Checklist. (The expectations listed in the figure are our examples from this chapter; you should replace them with your own.) Once your checklist is set up, use it to audit what you have on hand that will meet the reading and writing needs of your students and what learning tools you will be considering for purchase. Follow the same process for reading/language arts/English and for content areas. As we argue in Chapter 3, alignment is a necessary step in encouraging the wise use of instructional time and in creating an efficient curriculum system for which teachers can be held accountable.

But wait a minute! Are we advocating that you rush out and purchase all new materials? No, alignment is just the first factor to consider. Next, you must decide how will you know what materials to look for and how you will make objective decisions. How will you know if what you are currently using is just right as is? And if it's not, how will you know the modifications to make?

To answer these questions, use the information you have gathered to identify the literacy learning needs of your students (see Chapter 2). Say, for example, you have gifted, average, and reluctant readers and writers in your school. Perhaps some of your students are learning English as a second language and some are learning disabled. And many of your students seem to do well in language arts literacy, but struggle in science, mathematics, and social studies. Before you can determine which learning tools you need, you must be sure you can describe your *students'* strengths, weaknesses, and needs. To do this, analyze both standardized assessment data and teacher input. You may want your students to take a teacher-designed assessment that provides easy-to-understand data teachers can use to match students to texts, based on independent reading levels. Two widely used assessments you may decide to use are the Lexile Framework, designed by MetaMetrics, and Degrees of Reading Power, published by Touchstone Applied Science Associates, Inc.

Next, the Literacy Leadership Team or other designees will audit the learning tools currently used in your school and identify where you need to fill in the gaps with new, effective tools that will provide teachers with what they need to reach all students. Once this system is set up, it can continue to work for you. Experienced administrators know that teachers use the learning materials that are in their classrooms. Why, then, do so few school leaders participate in the selection process? Well, facing facts, teachers see interesting approaches or materials that they would like to use in their classrooms, and we want to support and motivate them to do this. So we say to teachers, "Sure, just see the bookkeeper and complete a purchase order. Let me know how it goes."

A far better approach is a more systematic one. Under the model we outline here, teachers and other personnel will bring information on materials they would like to try to the Literacy Leadership Team. The team will ask questions about each product, based on the classroom expectations for literacy and the criteria for literacy-focused learning tools. If a product meets the expectations and criteria *and* fits within the budget plan, then the decision would be to go ahead with the order.

This simple step may eliminate purchases that sit unused or that consume valuable learning time and do not show enough positive results for students. It not only allows teachers to have "ownership" of selections but also ensures that products selected meet the needs of the school and the students. We add one caveat: Because teachers come and go in schools, don't purchase any products that meet the approval of only one person. Make sure you have a consensus from the Literacy Leadership Team; otherwise, you could have a product that no one uses sitting on your shelves for the next 10 years. Deliberate, purposeful, objective selection of classroom materials is one of the most important steps in creating a fail-safe system of literacy within your school.

FIGURE 4.1
Effective Learning Tools Checklist

Directions: Depending on your school's organization, you may want to complete this checklist for each classroom, grade, or grouping in your school. In the first column, list your expectations for the reading/language arts/English classroom in your school. In the second column, identify the learning tools necessary to meet those expectations (we've provided samples based on the discussion in this chapter). In the third column, place a checkmark for learning tools currently used in the classroom. Blank space in the third column indicates there is a need for acquisition of a learning tool. In the fourth column, jot down your ideas for the purchase or use of learning tools.

Course Title: _____ Grade: _____

Teacher(s): _____

Expectations for Reading/ Language Arts/English Classrooms	Learning Tools Needed to Meet Expectations*	Learning Tools Now in Classrooms (✓)	Notes
Whole-Class Instruction	Anthology		
	– Diverse selections		
	– Ratio of fiction to nonfiction		
	– Integrates reading, writing, spelling, and grammar		
	Teacher Support		
	– Instructional strategies		
	– Second-language instruction		
	– Special education		
	– Applies to real world		
	– Higher-level thinking		
	– Web site/technical support		

TEMPLATE

FIGURE 4.1
(continued)

Course Title: _____ Grade: _____

Teacher(s): _____

Expectations for Reading/ Language Arts/English Classrooms	Learning Tools Needed to Meet Expectations*	Learning Tools Now in Classrooms (✓)	Notes
Small-Group Instruction	Teacher books – Reading comprehension – Reading strategies – Writing strategies Trade books – Thematic collections – Differentiated collections – Skill-building kits		
Accountable Independent Reading	Classroom library – Fiction: Various levels – Nonfiction: Various levels – Audiobooks – Compact disks		

*Examples

In the Classroom

It's the first day of the school year, and before the 7th grade students even enter their new language arts classroom, their eyes go to the stuffed "Dudley Do-Right" character taped to the door frame and the balloon note emerging from Dudley's mouth: "Bring a pencil!" The teacher, Cynthia, watches the students smile and elbow each other as they come in and find their seats. They begin nudging each other again as they absorb their visually stimulating and print-rich surroundings. Up front, there are three computers under a large sign reading "Tech Nest." Two other corners are marked "Author's Corner" and "Create and Connect." The fourth corner is outfitted with large pillows and lots and lots of books.

Cynthia greets the students and begins to outline what the daily routine will be. All of it will focus on reading and writing. She spends time building the classroom community of learners by asking each of them to tell about something they have read that they enjoyed or that relates to their life. Then she reads aloud a short book that has meaning for her: Kathleen Krull's *Wilma Unlimited,* about Olympic gold medalist Wilma Rudolph. The students discuss with Cynthia why the book has meaning for her. She says it motivates her to persevere, even in difficult times, and the students then say how they connected to it also. Then they use words and drawings to complete a sequence chart on what they heard. Next, they write adjectives on a stick figure to begin characterizing Wilma. The students are having fun, but when will they start working with all the resources they see?

Cynthia puts *Wilma* away and gives them an assignment: "Tomorrow, bring to class something you have enjoyed reading and I'll take your picture with it, and we'll make a bulletin board of literacy learners!"

A hand goes up, and Jay asks, "Do we get to do any of this stuff?" pointing to the Create and Connect Corner. Of course, Cynthia assures the students. This year, they'll be using many learning tools, including artistic ones, to express what they are learning and reading about. She explains that using different tools helps them to develop deeper knowledge and language for their writing (which they'll do in the Author's Corner).

Sensing the students' keen interest in knowing what will happen daily in class, Cynthia outlines the schedule and refers to the one posted on the board. "Each day we will read together or I'll read to you as I did with *Wilma* today. Then we will discuss and probably write a little to reflect on and understand more of what we have read and heard. We will always use language to express what we know and write about our reading. Next, we will work on the current unit, our grammar, and genres required in our standards. We'll use the stations for much of your independent work to make meaning of what we are learning."

Going over to the classroom library, Cynthia holds up a few of the books, calling out titles. She holds up *The House on Mango Street* by Sandra Cisneros and asks what they think the book is about. Students respond that it is about girls, Hispanic girls, and a street with mango trees. She reads Chapter 1 aloud and then places the book back in its place on the shelf. The students ask her to read more, but she replies, "Maybe one of *you* would like to read this book." Anna claims the book as hers, since it sounds like the place where she lives.

Cynthia watches the eyes of various students as they notice the variety of the library: magazines, trade books, fiction and nonfiction titles, and more. She realizes that to build fluency and become joyful, independent readers, students must practice reading, so she makes time for it in each day's schedule. Cynthia outlines accountable independent reading, telling students that they will be using reading logs and journals to document what they read and to record their reactions and responses to text and sentence prompts.

The students are ready for action! Cynthia can see they want to get involved with all the wonderful resources and possibilities this literacy-focused classroom holds. Having spent time setting up the physical environment, she now directs the students' attention to what will happen in this classroom regarding instruction. Cynthia knows from the Degrees of Reading Power (DRP) results and other data that her approach to instruction must include both whole-group and small-group instruction. She plans to use a variety of instructional strategies such as guided reading, read-alouds, think-alouds, and word study to guide student growth.

"Let's start with a book!" she says, holding up a copy of *Circle of Gold* by Candy Dawson Boyd. Every student has a copy of this book on his or her desk. Cynthia asks them to take a look at its cover, which shows a young girl smiling as she looks at several items in a jewelry case, and directs her students' attention to the cover caption: *It was the perfect gift. But was it enough to bring her family together again?* Before asking students what they think this gift is, Cynthia engages them in dialogue about which member of their family they would give a gift to, what they would give, and why. There are a number of responses (moms, dads, brothers, uncles, and cousins) and the gifts range from love and health to a house, jewelry, clothes, and money. The students' enthusiastic responses indicate they are engaged and interested in finding out more about the story.

Before they start reading, though, Cynthia takes time to introduce vocabulary and concepts that may prove challenging to students' comprehension of the text. From the list of words highlighted, students create flashcards with visual reminders of what each word means. There is chatter as students work in pairs to create flashcards and review the words. Cynthia reemphasizes the vocabulary and says that these words suggest strong feelings like frustration and anticipation.

The excitement seems to be mounting as Cynthia finally directs them to take a look at the first page of the book. Carefully creasing the page back, Cynthia begins reading the first three paragraphs aloud as the students read along silently. The last line she reads is *Mama had lost all interest in keeping the place neat.*

She proceeds to ask students to predict what they think the book will be about, based on what they've heard of the text so far or their prior knowledge. "What characters do we meet on this page?" Cynthia asks. "What's happening in her life? Based on what we've just learned, what kind of problem do you think is developing?" Students' answers are intriguing. They are interested and eager to find out what happens next . . . and whether their guesses are correct.

Cynthia's students follow along in their own copies as she reads the first chapter aloud, sharing strategies of expert readers: predicting, clarifying, summarizing, visualizing, questioning, and connecting. Then, the students write a one-sentence summary of the first chapter. Cynthia asks each student to share his or her sentence, and all do. Even the most reluctant readers in the group participate, because just one sentence is not too threatening.

And so the first day of class ends, with students believing that they will enjoy reading and learn to read and write better in Cynthia's class. She knows that creating a classroom for literacy started with creating a community of learners and respecting each student's interests, opinions, and ideas. By making clear what her expectations were of reading and writing, and carefully modeling strategies of expert readers and writers in a systematic approach, she began literacy learning. Students feel academically safe, knowing that this classroom system was set up for their success. Already, a sense of trust is developing. As the school year continues, they will experience a variety of reading materials and will use stations to write about their reading, reflect on it, and create new products based on it.

Review and reflection

Now, take a moment to review all the steps you have taken up to this point to develop a fail-safe system of literacy for your school. You have committed to literacy leadership and examined the commitment of the stakeholders in your school, district, and school community. You have examined data to determine the learning needs of the diverse students in your school. Alignment of curriculum, instruction, learning tools and assessment has provided a literacy system that will enhance the efficiency of the teachers' work and provide equal access for all students. Finally, you have created an expectation for the classroom for literacy, along with the commensurate learning tools. After taking these steps, we are sure you have figured out that many of your staff members will need support in making appropriate changes. You are now prepared to make objective decisions about how to provide the staff with what they need. Chapter 5 will help you design a professional development plan for your unique school.

Further reading in middle and high school literacy

Allen, J. (1995). *It's never too late: Leading adolescents to lifelong literacy.* Portsmouth, NH: Heinemann.

Allen, J. (1999). *Words, words, words: Teaching vocabulary in grades 4–12.* York, ME: Stenhouse Publishers.

Allen, J., & Gonzalez, K. (1998). *There's room for me here: Literacy workshop in the middle school.* York, ME: Stenhouse Publishers.

Beamon, G. W. (2001). *Teaching with adolescent learning in mind.* Arlington Heights, IL: SkyLight Professional Development.

Beers, K., & Samuels, B. G. (1998). *Into focus: Understanding and creating middle school readers.* Norwood, MA: Christopher-Gordon Publishers.

Billmeyer, R., & Barton, M. L. (1998). *Teaching reading in the content areas: If not me, then who?* Aurora, CO: McREL.

Brozo, W. G., & Simpson, M. L. (1999). *Readers, teachers, learners: Expanding literacy across the content areas* (3rd ed.). Upper Saddle River, NJ: Merrill.

Buehl, D. (2001). *Classroom strategies for interactive learning* (2nd ed.). Newark, DE: International Reading Association.

Donohue, P. L., Voekl, K. E., Campbell, J. R., & Mazzeo, J. (1999, March). *NAEP reading report card for the nation and states: Executive summary.* Available: http://nces.ed.gov/nationalreportcard/pubs/mail1998/199500html.

Harvey, S., & Goudvis, A. (2000). *Strategies that work: Teaching comprehension to enhance understanding.* York, ME: Stenhouse Publishers.

Keene, E. O., & Zimmermann, S. (1997). *Mosaic of thought: Teaching comprehension in a reader's workshop.* Portsmouth, NH: Heinemann.

Langer, J. A. (2000). *Achieving high quality reading and writing in an urban middle school: The case of Gail Slatko.* The National Center for English Language Learning & Achievement. Available: http://cela.albany.edu.

Marzano, R. J., Pickering, D. J., & Pollock, J. E. (2001). *Classroom instruction that works: Research-based strategies for increasing student achievement.* Alexandria, VA: Association for Supervision and Curriculum Development.

Routman, R. (1994). *Invitations: Changing teachers and learners K–12* (2nd ed.). Portsmouth, NH: Heinemann.

Stephens, E. C., & Brown, J. E. (2000). *A handbook of content literacy strategies: 75 practical reading and writing ideas.* Norwood, MA: Christopher-Gordon Publishers.

Taylor, R. (1999, December). Missing pieces: Aligned curriculum, instruction, and assessment. *Schools in the Middle, 9*(4), 14–16.

Taylor, R., Hasselbring, T. S., & Williams, R. D. (2001, October). Reading, writing, and misbehavior. *Principal Leadership, 2*(2), 34–39.

Tovani, C. (2000). *I read it, but I don't get it: Comprehension strategies for adolescent readers.* Portland, ME: Stenhouse Publishers.

Wilhelm, J. D. (2001). *Strategic reading guiding students to lifelong literacy, grades 6–12.* Portsmouth, NH: Boynton/Cook Publishers.

Wilson, E. (1999). *Reading at the middle and high school levels: Building active readers across the curriculum.* Arlington, VA: Educational Research Service.

5

Designing Professional
Development to Ensure Success

Now that you have committed to fail-safe literacy leadership, aligned your curriculum system, and created classroom expectations for literacy learning with identified learning tools, you are ready to ensure that the teachers have the knowledge and skills necessary for successful implementation. Throughout the process so far, you and your teachers have been learning more about adolescent literacy and the changes teachers can make in the classroom to enhance the success of students. Perhaps some teachers are already beginning to incorporate reading, writing, listening, speaking, viewing, and thinking into their instructional plans more consistently. Some teachers are probably asking for staff development on literacy strategies to use before, during, and after reading. Others are encouraging students to read independently and want to know how to motivate older reluctant readers. Still others are unsure of the expectations and are feeling anxious about the directive for all teachers to focus on literacy.

Implementing new curriculum, instructional strategies, classroom expectations, and learning tools does represent changes in daily practice within the school and can result in anxiety among the staff. One effective way to minimize negative responses to change is to ensure that teachers are involved in the processes. By collaboratively designing the professional development plan, perhaps with the Literacy Leadership Team or another representative group, stakeholders will feel more ownership over the change, leading to smoother implementation. This demonstrates in the process that the administrators are committed to teachers as an integral part in producing joyful, independent readers and writers.

Questions to guide professional development planning

Through many years of working with teacher and administrator groups to design professional development, we have found that using a series of guiding questions to stimulate thinking about their own experiences in professional growth facilitates productive planning. It also allows the group to build on the prior experience of their collaborators, so that everyone is operating with the same frame of reference. Think about your own professional growth as you review the guiding questions in Figure 5.1. Add your own responses to the example responses provided, which come from teachers and administrators who participated in some of our past professional development planning teams. (You won't be surprised to hear that the responses they gave are supported by research on the kinds of professional growth that boost student achievement.) Finally, use these guiding questions with your own team to open the planning session on your literacy-focused professional development.

Knowing that one-shot staff development does not improve the classroom experience of teachers or students, you will want to design a long-term, multi-year plan. Work collaboratively through the guiding questions to bring out background information to use in developing a professional development action plan—which will become your template for guiding the work of literacy leaders and instruction at every level.

Models for professional development

For the initial professional development experience, consider a kick-off event like an institute or mini-conference. You might bring in recognized specialists from a near-by university or nationally recognized consultants to provide motivational and content-rich presentations. Local experts, perhaps within your district or school, might lead smaller group sessions. Providing an initial experience that is attention getting, high quality and content rich sends faculty the message that this long-term professional development is to be taken seriously and is worth their time. It is particularly important to dispel teacher concerns and apprehensions relative to

TEMPLATE

FIGURE 5.1
Characteristics of Positive Professional Development

Directions: Think about the professional development experiences that made a positive impact on your teachers, and use those excellent examples to respond to the following guiding questions:

1. Who determined the results to be achieved?

   - ❖ *faculty planning groups*
   - ❖ *school improvement teams*
   - ❖ *principals and school administrators*

   - ❖ _____
   - ❖ _____
   - ❖ _____

2. Who determined the focus of the professional development?

   - ❖ *faculty groups*
   - ❖ *individuals who would be involved*
   - ❖ *resource teachers*
   - ❖ *principals and school administrators*

   - ❖ _____
   - ❖ _____
   - ❖ _____
   - ❖ _____

3. What kinds of professional development learning experiences have impacted your professional practice?

   - ❖ *those that were used the next day in class*
   - ❖ *those that gave the teachers experiences and practice similar to those to be given to students (National Writing Project)*
   - ❖ *those that took place over time*

   - ❖ *those that had collegial support (coaching, networking, study groups)*
   - ❖ _____
   - ❖ _____
   - ❖ _____

4. How did you know that professional development had a positive effect on student learning?

   - ❖ *students acted differently*
   - ❖ *students performed better*
   - ❖ *students wrote better*
   - ❖ *students read better*

   - ❖ _____
   - ❖ _____
   - ❖ _____
   - ❖ _____

5. What did leaders in your school/district do to make professional development successful?

   - ❖ *attended the sessions*
   - ❖ *provided release time*
   - ❖ *supported change with parents*
   - ❖ *purchased materials needed to implement the new ideas*

   - ❖ _____
   - ❖ _____
   - ❖ _____
   - ❖ _____

previous experiences with one-shot or fad approaches to professional growth that quickly fizzled and had no lasting impact. Note that in recommending an event, we are *not* suggesting that an event alone will meet your professional development needs. What it will do is establish staff awareness of overall expectations and other opportunities they can expect in the future.

Adults need choices in determining their professional growth, and we recommend you offer follow-up sessions for specific skill- and knowledge-enhancement through several channels. Examples might include study groups, action research, collegial classroom visits and coaching, and sharing sessions. Some schools hold weekly strategy sessions (offered during planning time and led by a school resource teacher) that build over the school year. Other schools offer professional development monthly in lieu of faculty meetings.

Whichever format or formats you select, be sure to provide both an initial focus and various follow-up sessions during the school year. With this strategy, "early adopters" and teacher-leaders can become the models and examples from whom others will learn over time. Essentially, you develop your own experts within the school. These individuals provide ongoing leadership for change and in doing so create a sense of ownership among their colleagues for new curriculum, instructional strategies, and learning tools as year one progresses and year two begins.

Here's an example of a successful professional development experience that resulted in improved reading and writing for students. When we were faced with design and implementation of a literacy intervention for middle school students reading below the 25th percentile, we knew that the teachers would have to do some things differently than they did in the past and that this would involve using new learning tools. Knowing that one-shot professional development would not improve the classroom experience for either teachers or students, we developed a multi-year plan based on developing teacher-leaders who would be role models for those coming on board after the first year.

During the first summer institute, we tapped national experts to guide the teachers, their principals, and district staff to an initial conceptual understanding of the planned literacy intervention and to show them how to get started. This approach—learning initially from the experts in the context of a classroom where the intervention would take place—combined the best of theory and practice. Putting teachers, administrators, and district staff in the classroom showed everyone how the classroom would be organized and allowed them to experience exactly what students and teachers would experience once school began. Principals' firsthand knowledge equipped them to be knowledgeable advocates to the entire faculty and to provide daily support to the pilot teachers.

Follow-up sessions were held about every six weeks to focus on smaller components of the intervention and to introduce or reinforce strategies that were appropriate for that particular time in the school year or "just in time." (We attributed a great deal of the success of the professional development to the concept of "just in time," which allows teachers to focus on small chunks of new information at the point of need.) These follow-up sessions always included time for problem solving and the sharing of effective practices.

In planning for the second-year expansion of the literacy intervention, the original teachers and principals became the primary teachers for new ones joining the project. Our goal was to develop teachers to assume the leadership role, to mentor, to network, to coach, and to assist each other in adopting new strategies for teaching and assessing students. In addition to strands for new teachers, we added strands for the experienced ones, for ESL teachers, and for special education teachers.

By developing a multi-year developmental plan focused on creating capacity for expansion, we were able to reach hundreds of teachers over a period of several years. Was this project successful? Well, measured reading achievement for students of project teachers grew consistently for four years running. What's more, the teachers loved the professional development and continued attending sessions even after the district reduced funds and could no longer provide compensation.

Here's another example, this time on a smaller scale. Recently, the principal of a high-achieving public high school in Orange County, Florida (a school that routinely puts up the highest SAT and ACT scores in the district) took a closer look at student test data and became concerned. Although the students' mean reading and writing scores were in the top quartile, that data showed that lots of students were struggling. When the principal observed classes, he saw many teachers using direct instruction—primarily lecturing—with follow-up reading and writing assignments. He wondered how the struggling students could manage to follow the lectures, read the text, and complete the writing assignments. The principal's subsequent discussions with the teachers confirmed what he had expected: The school was failing some of its most needy students, even though it was a model for high achievement!

The principal made a commitment to all students becoming joyful, independent readers and writers, communicated this commitment to his staff, and secured their commitment as well. He worked with a leadership team to implement a three-year course of study on adolescent literacy, focusing on literacy strategies. Today, a university consultant visits the school regularly to conduct workshops for teachers in their classrooms. A designated teacher-leader is responsible for coaching, providing regular faculty sharing sessions, study groups, and other ongoing assistance to teachers. As a result of this principal's fail-safe literacy leadership, teachers are using literacy strategies and struggling students are experiencing more success. On the state's accountability measure, students are already moving from the lower levels into the middle range.

Planning professional development to improve literacy

Based on our experience working with groups and individuals to implement successful programs like those you've just read about, we can recommend a five-step process for planning literacy-focused professional development:

1. Identify desired results.
2. Determine who will participate in professional development activities.
3. Identify components to achieve the desired results.
4. Plan for plan implementation.
5. Determine how you will recognize success.

Let's take a closer look at each step.

Step 1: Identify desired results

What specific results do you want and expect your professional development plan to achieve? One result might be improvements in reading or writing on a standardized measure for the school, for specific grade levels, or for subgroups of students. Another might be an increase in the number of accountable independent books students read each year. In the early days of plan implementation (before standardized test data is available), you might choose to look at teacher results like lesson plans, observations, and feedback on the effectiveness of the strategies they have learned through professional development activities. There are many other examples of outcomes or evidence you might select; those that you do select, however, must be both measurable and meaningful to the teachers who will be involved.

Step 2: Determine who will participate in professional development activities

Improving students' reading and writing is *everyone's* job. With this in mind, we recommend you incorporate a professional development component for everyone in the school for whom you've set a program expectation (see Chapter 4).

It's helpful to consider faculty in categories: the whole staff, reading/language arts/English teachers, content teachers, support personnel, administrators, and resource/curriculum teachers. The whole staff, for example, might benefit from an awareness session addressing the overall literacy plan and the level of intensity and expectations for the various groups of teachers. You'll probably want the language arts and reading teachers to participate in the most extensive reading and writing components. And content teachers should have a hefty amount of support in consistent implementation of literacy processes and literacy strategies. Finally, don't overlook the role of administrators. To leverage maximum benefit for students, administrators must play a role in writing the professional development plan and in the actual implementation. The principals of schools that show improvement in student achievement participate *with* their teachers in literacy-related professional development. This further reinforces the message that literacy is a priority and that the principal's actions make a difference.

Step 3: Identify components to achieve the desired results

You have identified the specific results you want to achieve and who will play a role. Now you need to think about the components of the professional development action plan that will assist the participants in achieving the desired results.

Begin by assembling your team to reflect on recently experienced professional development that targets the results you want to achieve. We recommend using the template in Figure 5.2 as a model. After noting these positive experiences, along with who can deliver a similar experience, the cost to the school, and the time requirements, you may find that your new action plan needs only to address gaps that remain in your current professional development plan. If your previous experiences have been good, you'll want to incorporate them in your orientation plan for newly hired staff members who don't have the same background.

After careful review of the best experiences, you and your team are ready to consider new and different ones. List each group of participants (whole staff, reading/language arts/English teachers, content teachers, etc.), identify components to target the desired results, determine who will be responsible for the component, determine how its effects will be measured, and provide an estimate of the component's fiscal impact. Figure 5.3 provides an example. Note that the figure includes how the results will be measured, but leaves a blank space for actual gains; these would be filled in when the gains become apparent, later in the school year. Also note that some of the "when" column is specific and some is open ended because it is yet to be decided.

By now, you're probably wondering who is going to be responsible for seeing the details of this professional development plan worked out, consultant arrangements made, teachers communicated with, substitutes arranged for, and the budget adhered to. Specifically, you're probably wondering, "Must it be *me?*"

Of the schools we have worked with, those that have consistent reputations for being on the cutting edge all have a well-informed designee responsible for overseeing professional growth. This person, who has more than a full-time job, is very seldom an administrator; usually, he or she is a resource teacher at the school—a respected colleague capable of coaching others in a respectful way and willing to conduct demonstration classes and model strategies in other teachers' classrooms and during weekly forums. For schools that are committed to all students becoming joyful, independent readers and writers, this position is a must.

TEMPLATE

FIGURE 5.2
Analysis of Past Professional Development

Directions: Use this template to assist you in reviewing recent professional development experiences to identify those that were excellent, those that overlapped (so you can streamline), those that were consistent (supportive of one another), and gaps in professional development (so you can plan to address them).

Best Previous Topics/Experiences (Over Past 2–3 Years)	Overlap (Duplications and Links)	Consistencies (Common Topics & Themes)	Gaps (Topics/ Resources Missing)

	EXAMPLE			
FIGURE 5.3 **A Professional Development Action Plan**				
Who	**What**	**When**	**How**	**Evaluation**
Whole Staff	Literacy is Everyone's Job! (literacy processes, strategies, accountable independent reading)	Summer Institute	$5000 School Improvement	Participant feedback Review of lesson plans
Language Arts/English Teachers	Study Group Reading I: *It's Never Too Late* (Allen, 1995) Study Group Reading II: Teachers' Selection—TBD	August– November January– May	$150 $150	Classroom changes Student grades Teacher feedback
Reading Teachers	Monthly Strategy Sessions Resources: *Teaching Reading in the Content Areas: If Not Me, Then Who?* (Billmeyer & Barton, 1998) *Strategies That Work: Teaching Comprehension to Enhance Understanding* (Harvey & Goudvis, 2000).	Every Wednesday, during planning	$100 District and publisher consultants	Lesson plans Teacher observations
Math Teachers	Quarterly literacy strategy sessions to improve test results	August–May	None	Test results
Language Arts/Reading Teachers	Accountable independent reading strategies	September 8	$2000 Substitutes Publisher's consultant	Number of books students read
Content Area Teachers	Strategy series Resource: *A Handbook of Content Literacy Strategies* (Stephens & Brown, 2000)	September– May Fourth Wednesday planning session	$300	Lesson plans Observation Feedback Participation
Administrators	Attend strategy sessions and participate in study groups	August–May	None	Comparison of pre/post knowledge Coaching
Whole Faculty	Online courses: Commercial or Florida On-line Reading Professional Development	August–May	Cost TBD District purchase?	Participant feedback Course completion rates
Selected Faculty	Conference and institute attendance	August–May	$5000	Presentations to faculty Instructional changes

Step 4: Plan for plan implementation

In our experience, schools that take the extra time to plan for the strategic implementation of their professional development action plans avoid pitfalls that can slow progress and even derail best intentions. Before you sign off on your plan, sit down with your team to identify potential problems and their likely solutions. Fail-safe literacy leadership includes planning for success and intervening when necessary.

First, garner district support for your plan, both financially and verbally, in the event that questions from teachers or parents rise to that level. The best insurance for district support is communication throughout the development process. Through careful communication, we were successful in working with schools to fund extra days for new and veteran teachers to participate in professional development.

Second, lay the foundation for positive communication throughout your school. This is absolutely critical, because in reality, not everyone will be excited about the opportunity for professional growth. Keep the entire faculty informed throughout the planning process and seek input from grade-level and content area groups and through focus groups. What your staff members really want and need to know is when each of them will be expected to participate and if compensation or release time will be available. Be sure to provide answers to these questions up front.

In working with some districts, we have found hundreds of teachers who say they would attend respected institutes on their own time and feel special doing so. On the other hand, when meeting at a national principal's organization with a nationally representative planning group, we heard an urban representative state unequivocally that no teacher would attend any kind of professional development during the summer—paid or not. Knowing that school and district cultures differ, you must find a way to make the professional development plan as attractive as possible to your unique faculty. As principals, if given a choice, neither of us would consider hiring a teacher candidate who didn't have a history of participating in professional development and who would not make the commitment to participate.

Finally, remember to present new professional development requirements in a positive light. When it comes time to present the completed professional development plan to your staff, do so in a collegial setting and at the same time that you present the school's annual improvement plan. There should be no surprises, as everyone should have had input and insight along the way. Still, you should respond to questions and assure your staff that the plan will be "tweaked" as needed. Even the very best printed plan is useless when no one attends to it; for this reason, the climate of its presentation is critical to inspire strong faculty participation and follow through.

Step 5: Determine how you will recognize success

When it comes to professional development, recognizing success may not be as simple as we think. Generally, at the end of in-service training, participants rate the presenter on items like preparation, quality of materials, accomplishing objectives, and delivery. Immediate feedback of this type is important to the presenter, helping to improve the quality and delivery of the next presentation. This kind of feedback is also important to the funding or credit-granting body, which may require it. And certainly, this information can help you determine if you want to use a particular consultant again. However, these end-of-session evaluations will not tell you what you really need to know: the impact this training will have on student learning.

Recognizing success of your professional development action plan requires another type of measure, focused on changes in student performance, attitude, and behavior. Teacher attitude and instructional strategy may also be reflected. You may see changes in lesson plans a long time before you see changes in student grades and achievement data (which take more than a year).

> **Rose:** *When working with school and districts, I often receive feedback first from administrators who have observed changes in teachers, then in students. Soon after, teachers will begin sharing with me instructional plans that model literacy processes and strategies.*

Developing a plan to monitor the progress of the professional development and make changes as needed is insurance. Don't wait until the end of the school year to find out how things are going. Attend professional development sessions personally and talk with teachers about what they are learning. Reinforce the learning through visits to classrooms, reviews of lesson plans and talks with students. Research tells us that principals providing instructional leadership spend a lot of time providing for professional development and talking with teachers about their daily work related to professional development. Even these types of casual, seemingly insignificant discussions reinforce the importance of literacy and reassure teachers that their administration supports their efforts to help all students become joyful, independent readers and writers.

As the first year of implementation draws to a close, be sure to provide feedback on the successes to date and the strategies to be modified. Reflection on what has worked and what has not worked will provide you with the template for year two expansion. Deliberate and purposeful input, feedback, and communication with the staff and all stakeholders will assist everyone in understanding that the commitment is long term and unwavering.

Professional development within a community of learners

If this heading looks familiar, it should! In Chapter 4, we stressed that creating the community of learners is vital for maximizing student success, and much the same holds true for optimizing the professional growth of faculties and staffs. We want to develop a school culture that expects professional growth and has a sense of safety, choice, and motivation to participate and implement the strategies being learned. When teachers encounter challenges or meet with limited success, they should feel comfortable sharing experiences and asking for support. In the subsections that follow, we share effective strategies for creating community that you and your team might consider.

Strategy 1: Ask teacher-leaders to serve as trusted colleagues

Earlier in this chapter, we raised the idea of having a designee responsible for carrying out the details of planning and implementing professional development and measuring its results. These administrative tasks are critical for translating a paper plan into live action; however, functionality alone won't ensure success. Emotional engagement with ideas, materials, and colleagues will take positive results of professional development to a higher level. Likewise, the odds of higher-level results are improved when professional development is led by a caring, esteemed, knowledgeable colleague who can establish the degree of trust necessary to persuade teachers to "risk" making changes in the classroom.

So allow us to underscore our case for establishing a literacy resource teacher position to facilitate both formal and informal literacy learning. This teacher-leader has hallway and in-class discussions related to the nuances of incorporating strategies or motivating individual learners to step up to the expectations. This person listens and empathizes with teachers who are frustrated over their struggle to reach every student, but continually encourages them with coaching and feedback. This invaluable teacher will also attend to the necessary tasks of ordering materials and subscriptions and arranging the "administrivia" necessary for successful professional development sessions.

Like many school districts throughout the United States, in recent years ours had to make several personnel cutbacks to offset financial shortfalls. During this period, the middle and high schools in our district that continued to make steady progress (as measured by state assessments) eliminated other positions, but they *never* cut their literacy resource teacher positions. The schools that did eliminate these positions quickly learned the value of the service those teachers provided and reinstated the positions as soon as possible. We encourage you to provide for such a teacher-level position—whether you call it the literacy resource teacher, the curriculum or literacy coach, or another title.

Strategy 2: Set up a special place for professional development

When something is really important, we provide a special place for it. Set aside space for a formal professional development resource center. The space need not be large, but it needs to be there—and the closer to the center of the school you can locate it, the stronger the message you will send.

The most effective professional development spaces we have seen incorporate the office of the literacy resource teacher and an area for professional development sessions. The space should be professional, not cutesy, as we sometimes find in schools. The furniture should be designed for adults, not for students. Trapezoidal, circular, or half-width rectangular tables are useful, as they can be rearranged depending upon the number of participants and learning strategy used. Ideally, the space will reflect your school's expectation of a classroom for literacy learning. When set up for functionality and used consistently, a professional development resource center can become the focal point for your school's reading and writing improvement efforts.

Strategy 3: Provide a variety of resources for independent and group use

In the special place you set aside for professional development, faculty and staff should find a plethora of resources reflecting a diversity of interests and professional maturity. Books for both the beginning teacher and the seasoned veteran should abound. Stock single copies of some books and multiple copies of others in quantities large enough for study groups. Consider ordering special selections for the entire faculty to stimulate discussions and lay groundwork for particular professional development sessions. You may want to review the "further reading" sections at the end of each of this book's chapters to assist you in developing an order list.

You'll also need subscriptions to professional journals that combine theory and practice. One principal we know always had the journals routed to him before they were placed in the professional development resource center. He selected particularly appropriate pieces and referenced them in weekly communiqués with the faculty. Another principal had the habit of inserting gift certificates and dollar bills in journals to mark especially good articles. These techniques let the faculty know that professional reading was important and therein they would find rewards!

Your professional development resource center should also incorporate technology resources. Teachers should have online access to curriculum, instructional strategies, and research. The center also provides a good environment to try out and evaluate sample teacher software. In thinking about technology, don't forget the technology necessary for delivery of professional development. Basic equipment includes projection devices for the computer, an overhead projector, speakers, a large television, and a VCR. By providing up-to-date resources in the center, you will find that it will become a place for collegial research, discussion, and growth.

Strategy 4: Budget for maximum participation

When you are budgeting for your professional development action plan, you will also want to provide financial support for the professional development resource center and for the literacy resource teacher. Use these funds to purchase materials, provide release time for in-school coaching, provide opportunities to visit other schools and other teachers, and cover conference registration and travel costs.

Nothing reinforces a teacher's sense of professionalism like attending a state or national education conference. Sending teams to a targeted conference to search out the best ideas and design plans for implementation is often money well spent, particularly if an administrator is part of the team. Recently, we organized a national institute on literacy and restricted attendance to teams of teachers accompanied by their principals. The feedback was tremendous, and we easily met our attendance goal. This experience confirms that we should not shy away from creating expectations that are correct (such as principals should attend professional development with teachers) just because they depart from the norm in secondary schools.

A note on new technology's role in professional development

Another way to provide faculty with quality professional growth experiences is through time-flexible online courses and services, some of which can be accessed for free and some of which are available for purchase. There are lots of options out there; of course, we must remind ourselves, just as we would remind our students, that unless the source is a credible one, the information may be faulty. You must do your research.

When it comes time to decide which reputable online professional development services to select for your staff, consider both efficiency and effectiveness. Preview a variety and compare them with your answers to the original guiding questions and your professional development action plan. Some questions to ask the provider include

- ❖ How do the online courses incorporate the principles of adult learning?
- ❖ How do you provide for modeling of strategies?
- ❖ Is there any face-to-face support provided?
- ❖ How much interaction in "real time" is available?
- ❖ What are the course completion rates?

❖ What impact on student achievement and teacher instruction has been documented?

❖ Who are the *actual instructors* (as contrasted with faculty members and program advisors)?

If you do decide to incorporate online courses in your professional development action plan, make sure that someone will be able to provide support within your school. Remember that those of us in education tend to value relationships and like to interact with others during the learning process. Perhaps realizing this, when Florida launched a new series of reading-focused online professional development available free to its certified teachers, the state also provided guidelines for facilitators and study groups. Just like face-to-face learning experiences, some manner of follow up, whether it's study groups or collegial coaching, is essential to maximize the impact of online courses.

A reality check

So perhaps you are wondering, "*Will* designing professional development with my team be as easy as 1–2–3?" Absolutely not, and it is not our intent to paint such a picture. We are not looking through rose-colored glasses or advising you to do so. Thanks to our own experience, we are the first to realize the tremendous work involved.

As a middle school principal, Valerie found the first indication that her school's professional development plan was working not in student achievement, but in faculty attitudes and actions. First and foremost, she noticed changes in how they perceived themselves and their students. Ideas began to spark other ideas as teachers discussed what they were reading, practicing, and perfecting in their classrooms. Slowly, the infinite potential of what they could achieve with students began to dawn.

Valerie: *Teachers started leaving notes in my mailbox and popping into my office with invitations to participate in a classroom activity, observe a new strategy, or celebrate an achievement toward our schoolwide literacy goals. I also noticed that teachers had begun collaborating, rather than working in isolation. The media center, where we had set up a special place for professional development, became a hangout for troubleshooting and rehearsing* *concepts and ideas as teachers convened to strategize ways to integrate what they were learning. One group of teachers even sought advanced degrees to extend their knowledge and skills for reaching our most challenging students.*

Rose: *I had a similar experience at the district level. When we designed our literacy intervention, The Orange County Literacy Project, initially, we could not find teachers willing to take on the most needy students. But after the first year, when news of the professional development and support had begun to spread, along with news of the unheard of turn-around students were making, teachers began calling me and saying "I want to be a Literacy Project teacher. Can you help me get a position?"*

Both these experiences are typical. Once teachers in Valerie's school had experienced how motivating success with new literacy strategies could be, their thirst for knowledge became insatiable. Once teachers in Rose's district saw the kind of success they could achieve, they were anxious to take on the challenge. However, please note that these things didn't happen overnight. They came about thanks to continued, ever-present literacy leadership and support from teacher-leaders and the district leadership.

In the Classroom

Karen is teaching a lesson in a 7th grade physical science classroom. It's a particularly important lesson because it covers science concepts and at the same time, teaches, models, and practices literacy strategies. Today's strategy involves using sticky notes to practice predicting, questioning, clarifying, visualizing, connecting, and summarizing. Karen found the idea in Harvey and Goudvis's *Strategies That Work* (2000).

The first thing Karen does is pass out a contemporary article related to the science standards in the current unit, pads of small sticky notes, and a handout identifying six strategies of expert readers. She asks the students to predict what the article is about by looking at the picture clues, headings, and boldface type. She engages their prior knowledge on the content topic at hand. Then she instructs them on the six strategies of expert readers and asks them to use each strategy at least once while reading the article. What is unusual is that she asks the students to use the sticky notes to write down each time they use a particular strategy (questioning, clarifying, etc.) and stick it right there on the page! As adults, we often write on a page in a text, but students are forbidden to do so. Sticky notes allow and encourage students to take notes right when and where they want to, helping them to comprehend text while maintaining momentum.

The students follow Karen's directions and begin their reading and "sticky note-taking." *All* the students are busy reading and writing. They like this change of pace. It is better than reading and answering questions or preparing an outline (which most never complete). When finished, they pair up to discuss how they used the strategies and the science content they just read. After a few minutes, Karen facilitates a discussion, inviting students to share when, where, and how they used particular strategies *and* the science content they learned in the process. Students also share how much they like using the sticky notes!

After the class, Karen meets with Jim, the physical science teacher, to debrief about the lesson. That's right: Karen is *not* the science teacher; she's the school's literacy resource teacher, responsible for facilitating literacy learning and professional development activities. As a trusted colleague, she models strategies for enhancing literacy and content learning in other teachers' classrooms and with other teachers' students.

Jim tells Karen that he is amazed at the degree of participation his students showed and at the depth of their discussion. He also notes that with both their heads and their hands engaged, students were too busy to misbehave! More than that, he saw students who had not done much all year long really working hard. Jim tells Karen that seeing his own students perform more consistently with rigorous and relevant content has made a believer of him. He vows to try the sticky note strategy again and to continue to ask Karen to support him in his teaching. As Karen leaves the physical science classroom, she offers to lend Jim a copy of *Teaching Reading in the Content Areas: If Not Me, Then Who?* (Billmeyer & Barton, 1998), a great resource on teaching and using literacy strategies.

Review and reflection

As a literacy leader, ensuring the success of your school's professional development plan is not easy. Some teachers will resent your requests to attend sessions, to work collaboratively, and to monitor and adapt to student progress. Members of your staff may approach professional development not with excitement, but with apprehension of unwelcome change. Throughout the process, you will remind them of your common goal for all students to become joyful, independent readers and writers. With patience and consistency, your literacy leadership will spark positive changes in both teachers and students.

Further reading in professional development

Billmeyer, R., & Barton, M. L. (1998). *Teaching reading in the content areas: If not me, then who?* Aurora, CO: McRel.

Blase, J., & Blase, J. (2001). *Empowering teachers: What successful principals do.* Thousand Oaks, CA: Corwin.

Harvey, S., & Goudvis, A. (2000). *Strategies that work: Teaching comprehension to enhance understanding.* York, ME: Stenhouse.

Joyce, B., & Showers, B. (2002). *Student achievement through staff development* (3rd ed.). Alexandria, VA: Association for Supervision and Curriculum Development.

Little, J. W. (1993, Summer). Teachers' professional development in a climate of educational reform. *Educational Evaluational Policy Analysis, 15*(2), 129–152.

Taylor, R. (2001, Fall). Teacher's challenge. *Journal of Staff Development, 22*(4), 56–59.

6

Building Capacity for Continuous Improvement

By THIS STAGE IN THE PROCESS, YOU AND YOUR FACULTY HAVE SPENT MONTHS with your school faculty studying, planning, and preparing for implementation of a fail-safe system of literacy that will ensure all students the opportunity to become joyful, independent readers and writers. Through your literacy leadership, you have analyzed stakeholders' commitment level to all students and influenced the commitment of those whose beliefs weren't consistent with yours. With your staff and your Literacy Leadership Team, you have disaggregated and studied data to determine who is learning literacy behaviors satisfactorily and who is not. Using this data to drive your decisions, you have perhaps rethought your school's organization and its allocation of time and resources so that you're able to serve every student in an optimal way.

Close examination of the extent of alignment of standards, curriculum, instruction, learning tools, and assessment has helped you and your leadership team make decisions regarding what essential skills, concepts, and content students will learn, *how* they will learn, and what learning tools classroom teachers will use. Then, with your Literacy Leadership Team, you applied recent research on how students acquire and develop literacy behaviors to create carefully considered expectations for literacy-focused classrooms. All these objective processes helped you to encourage staff members to begin to use literacy processes and literacy strategies and to eliminate unproductive practices. Finally, you led the creation of a professional development plan that will support all staff members in developing the knowledge and skills to effectively support every learner. What else could possibly be needed?

Only this: The promise of continuous growth and improvement. Once the decisions have been made and professional development begun, other influences may distract you from keeping the vision on a daily basis. As the literacy leader, your final but enduring responsibility is to build the capacity for ongoing growth in literacy behaviors.

While the time for studying and planning has been difficult, sustaining the momentum and commitment and taking action can be an even greater challenge. Think about completing your fail-safe system of literacy with these processes to provide ongoing vision-keeping, support, and accountability for achieving the ultimate goal of all students becoming joyful, independent readers and writers:

1. Create an action plan for a fail-safe system of literacy.
2. Identify roles and responsibilities for literacy, and select, reflect, and reward personnel with literacy in mind.
3. Celebrate successes!

Create an action plan for a fail-safe system of literacy

Over the period of time that you have been applying the concepts and taking the steps outlined in this book's first five chapters, you have been developing your school's action plan for a fail-safe system of literacy. Some of the steps you have taken by yourself; some you have taken in collaboration with your Literacy Leadership Team. Meet now with your Literacy Leadership Team to develop, implement, and evaluate a formal action plan for your school's fail-safe system of literacy. This action plan may also become a portion of your school improvement plan.

Your school's literacy action plan will be unique to your school community's needs, but will probably include some common sections. In the next few pages, we address six sections you'll definitely want to incorporate in your action plan:

❖ A statement of the school's belief in and commitment to all students becoming joyful, independent readers and writers
❖ A data-driven discussion targeting who is not learning literacy behaviors

❖ An action plan for resolving curriculum system discrepancies
❖ A guide for the ideal literacy-focused classroom
❖ A professional development action plan
❖ Feedback measures for monitoring plan effectiveness

Section 1: A statement of the school's belief in and commitment to all students becoming joyful, independent readers and writers

This statement should be fairly brief and include commitments that you have made (see Chapter 1) and the actions that you will take. An example of the belief and commitment statement might be something like this:

> Jones Middle School believes that every student will become a joyful, independent reader and writer before the end of 8th grade. Our commitment to this belief will be demonstrated by prioritizing literacy as number one when making decisions, particularly decisions regarding negotiable uses of time, personnel, and resources.

Section 2: A data-driven discussion targeting who is not learning literacy behaviors

This discussion should be brief and based on the study of data and classroom evidence that you have collected and analyzed (see Chapter 2). Clarity regarding who is learning literacy behaviors at a level that is satisfactory and who is not will ensure that the literacy action plan you develop will meet the needs of targeted students. Here's an excerpt from a data-driven discussion focused on improving mathematics achievement through literacy improvement:

> At Jones Middle School, 8th grade student mean scores for mathematics computation are in the 65th percentile. On the other hand, the 8th grade mean percentile for solving word problems is in the 44th percentile. This indicates that in grades 6–8, we need to target mathematics vocabulary, reading comprehension, and analysis to help our students solve word problems. When we look at students who score below the school mean, we find that our English language learners comprise about half of those students. The data tells us that in addition to targeting problem solving for all students, we need to address academic language of mathematics and look at alignment of learning tools, time allocation, and literacy strategies for our English language learners.

The data-driven discussion targeting who is not learning literacy behaviors (in this case, 8th grade mathematics students and particularly those who are English language learners) links directly to the next section of your action plan, where the discrepancies in alignment will be identified and action items written. In the excerpt provided, we see that Jones Middle School's 8th graders performed well in mathematics computation, but floundered with problem solving. The discrepancy is between the standards-based curriculum (which includes word problem solving) and the instructional strategies the teachers are currently using, which do not sufficiently address the literacy skills students need to solve word problems.

Section 3: An action plan for resolving curriculum system discrepancies

This section should list action items for resolving all discrepancies identified. Some action items for Jones Middle School might be to require mathematics teachers to incorporate literacy strategies before, during, and after reading to help students understand what word problems are asking them to do, the vocabulary of mathematics, how to find clues within a word problem's language that will help them formulate a solution strategy, and ways to check if their answers make sense. This action plan might also address the professional development and learning tools the mathematics teachers would need to help them teach these literacy skills.

For your school's Section 3, try using your filled-in Curriculum System Alignment template (Figure 3.1, page 41) as the basis. For each category (curriculum, instructional strategies, learning tools, assessment, professional development), create an actionable item to resolve the discrepancy identified between "What Is" and "What Should Be." These items should also address the targeted needs of students who are not learning literacy satisfactorily, identified in Section 2. Figure 6.1 shows an excerpt from such an action plan; it should give you additional ideas for developing your own.

Section 4: A guide for the ideal literacy-focused classroom

This section is based on the specific classroom expectations for literacy learning behaviors that you want to see from teachers and students. For a resource, you consult the Effective Learning Tools Checklist (see Figure 4.1, page 78) you developed, which identifies the tools your school will need

EXAMPLE

FIGURE 6.1
Action Plan for Resolving Curriculum System Discrepancies (Excerpt)

Component	Discrepancy	Action	Who	When	Cost
Curriculum	Fluency with nonfiction	Teach nonfiction: Increase proportion of nonfiction reading from 10% to 50%	Language arts teachers and content area teachers	2nd quarter	n/a
		Use literacy strategies to develop vocabulary, concepts, and content knowledge to improve problem solving results	Mathematics teachers	All year	n/a
Instructional Strategies	Fluency with nonfiction	Read alouds	Language arts teachers	All year	n/a
		Shared and independent reading	Content area teachers		
Learning Tools	Fluency with nonfiction	Purchase nonfiction (specifically, books for independent reading on content standards).	Media Specialists	March	$10,000
		Select anthologies, core text with higher proportion of literacy strategies	Department chairs select books for content areas		
Assessment	Fluency with nonfiction	Practice comprehension assessment and writing prompts	All teachers	October–March	n/a

before teachers can fully implement classrooms that enhance literacy learning. (Note that those learning tool needs are also included in Figure 6.1.)

Now, for Section 4 of your action plan, take the same specific classroom expectations that you believe to be ideal and create a classroom guide for literacy. This guide will serve as a starting point for your school's new literacy efforts. Later, you may want to develop a rubric similar to the one in Figure 6.2, which allows for distinctions in the levels of implementation; however, the guide you create now will be a valuable resource for consistent implementation and growth in literacy behaviors, in that you and your faculty can use it for self-assessment, for coaching, for goal setting, and for discussions centered on helping every student to become a joyful, independent reader and writer. Some principals may also want to share the guide (and eventually, the rubric) with parents so they will know what type of instructional strategies to expect in their children's classrooms. Sharing with parents, we should note, raises the level of accountability for teachers.

Figure 6.2 and Figure 6.3 provide two samples created for the Different Ways of Knowing Middle Grades Comprehensive School Reform model. The first is a rubric focused on a classroom environment that supports literacy learning; the second is a classroom guide showing both student and teacher literacy behaviors. There are many benefits to be gained from these two resources. They reinforce common classroom expectations for literacy. They serve as a guide for professional goal setting, coaching, and professional development. Both are excellent tools for reflection—especially for literacy leaders looking to support teachers' literacy-boosting efforts.

Section 5: A professional development action plan

After reviewing the data on who is learning literacy behaviors and who is not, planning to eliminate discrepancies in your curriculum system alignment, and creating a classroom guide or rubric to use as a tool for improving classroom practice, you are ready to review and formalize the professional development action plan you have been developing (see Chapter 5). Ask yourself the following questions:

❖ Does the plan address the highest priority needs?
❖ Does the plan address the learning needs that will emerge from curriculum alignment?

❖ Does the plan address learning needs that will emerge from incorporating aligned learning tools?

❖ Does the plan address learning needs that will emerge from the expectations set in the ideal literacy classroom guide/rubric?

Revise your professional development action plan based on your answers to these questions.

Section 6: Feedback measures for monitoring plan effectiveness

Writing plans for improvement is not the end of fail-safe literacy leadership. We are embroiled in accountability, and no accountability is more important than accountability for increasing literacy. The key to making the action items in this plan fail-safe is to build in ongoing feedback. By continually seeking input through surveys, focus groups, class visits and (eventually) hard data, you will always be adjusting the action plan, moving it closer and closer to your goal.

Based on the data you studied, the discrepancies you found and are addressing, and the classroom rubric you created, identify and formalize within the finished action plan a list of easily accessible means of getting feedback on the plan's effectiveness. First, determine what evidence and benchmarks you will accept that the plan is or is not working. Second, determine how you will gather this evidence. Third, decide how you will provide feedback and make adjustments to the action plan based on the evidence that you receive.

Evidence of the action plan's success or additional needs may include findings to questions such as these:

❖ Do teachers' instructional plans identify standards, literacy strategies, assessment techniques, and learning tools that support this action plan?

❖ When walking through the school, is it apparent that the plan is in place?

❖ Has a commitment been made to find time for accountable independent reading?

❖ Are teachers requesting more materials for independent reading, read-alouds, and shared reading?

❖ How does book circulation in the media center compare now with one year ago?

TEMPLATE

FIGURE 6.2
Classroom Rubric for Literacy Learning

Teacher_____   Date_____

Directions: Self-monitoring the literacy elements in your Different Ways of Knowing classroom will help you identify areas for growth and celebration. Check where you think you are on the continuum from novice to role model. You may want to ask for feedback from a colleague.

Different Ways of Knowing:
A Middle-Grades School Classroom Rubric for Literacy

Classroom Environment	Novice (coming to know)	Proficient (showing you know)	Role Model (knowing you know)	Comments
Literacy- and print-rich				
Small-group instruction area				
Centers: Reading, writing/ expression, technology, independent reading				
Attractive, risk-free, safe				
Smooth schedule and groups, transitions				
Student-known routines, resources				
Maximized time for literacy learning				
Integrated content, standards-based planning				
Use of before, during, and after reading literacy strategies				
Art infusion to assess, deepen, and express knowledge				
Integration of test taking strategies				
Promotion of teamwork and critical thinking				

FIGURE 6.2
(continued)

Celebration of literacy learning is apparent				
Technology for learning and expression				
Reading	**Novice (coming to know)**	**Proficient (showing you know)**	**Role Model (knowing you know)**	**Comments**
Model joy of reading to/with students daily				
Include accountable independent reading daily				
Assist students in selecting books to read				
Teach grammar, spelling, etc., in context				
Promote reading nonfiction				
Focus discussions on critical thinking				
Monitor reading for improvement				
Writing				
Integrate writing with reading				
Model writing to/with students				
Assign writing daily for variety of meaningful purposes				
Teach writing as a process with multiple drafts				
Use writing to promote critical thinking				
Teach writing conventions in context				
Provide choice in writing				
Use writing to exceed content standards				

EXAMPLE

FIGURE 6.3
A Classroom Guide for Literacy Learning

Teachers who are experts at literacy learning create an optimal setting for learning, assist their students in owning strategies of good readers, and provide for independent reading. Please use "Literacy Learning *at a Glance*" to synthesize what you see as you visit classrooms or as points of inquiry in coaching colleagues.

Literacy Learning *at a Glance*

What are teachers doing?	What are students doing?
Creating a Setting for Learning Management Strategies Teachers Use	**Responding to the Setting for Learning** Behaviors Students Exhibit
Provide for print rich environment.	Access a variety of sources for reading.
Arrange the classroom for differentiated instruction (small-group, independent work, centers, etc.).	Change learning activity about every 15 minutes. Work in groups, independently, and alone with the teacher.
Plan for routines, use of resources, groups, and transition times.	Know routines, access and maintain materials, change groupings smoothly, respect teacher and other students during transition times.
Structure learning with before, during and after literacy strategies. Classroom organization relates to managing materials, activities, and hence learning.	Anticipate and generate connections to prior knowledge, other texts, and classes. Begin to develop own strategies, organizers, and meta-cognitive reflections.
Develop learning events that relate reading to writing and use writing to enhance reading.	Write about what they read, their thoughts and feelings, their experiences, and what they observe.
Develop learning events that incorporate all literacy processes: reading, writing, speaking, listening, viewing and expressing.	Draw, model, act, read, write, create, and express in a variety of ways their understanding of concepts.
Create a classroom community that is physically safe, psychologically safe, and academically safe.	Take risks by asking questions, asking for feedback, and sharing ideas openly. Respect the teacher and each other.
Owning Strategies of Good Readers Instructional Processes Teachers Use	**Owning Strategies of Good Readers** Cognitive Processes Students Use
Teach literacy strategies explicitly.	Develop and apply strategies of good readers.
Access prior knowledge through writing, speaking, arts infusion, multiple symbol systems.	Make connections to what they already know, and have read.

EXAMPLE	
FIGURE 6.3 *(continued)*	
Owning Strategies of Good Readers Instructional Processes Teachers Use	**Owning Strategies of Good Readers** Cognitive Processes Students Use
Model and teach question/answer relationships Practice/encourage questioning.	Ask questions about what they read, the author, and of themselves.
Model and teach strategies during & after reading.	Draw inferences, conclusions, and make applications during and after reading.
Teach concepts of print and text, particularly nonfiction/informational text. Teach how to use specific content texts.	Distinguish between important and less important information; note taking, highlighting, outlining, etc.
Model and teach strategies for organizing information, synthesizing information (graphic organizers, webbing, think-alouds, KWL, structured note taking, etc.).	Synthesize information within and across texts. Understand relationships among different works and experiences.
Monitor comprehension of independent, shared, and class readings.	Check for understanding and correct misunderstanding when reading. Ask, "Does this make sense?"
Creating Independent Readers How Teachers Motivate Independent Reading	**Becoming an Independent Reader** What Students Do to Develop Fluency
Assess independent reading levels.	Select reading that is "just right."
Provide reading materials that are respectful of age and diversity of students.	Relate to the characters and context of the book.
Monitor growth by holding students accountable.	Write reading logs, journals, book advertisements or other feedback for the teacher.
Model the joy of reading: read-alouds, anticipatory reading.	Conference with teacher and peers about books.
Strategically promote reading: literature circles, book pass, etc.	Volunteer to promote favorite books, genres, authors, and characters.

❖ Who has been attending professional development and implementing strategies learned?

❖ How does measurable achievement in reading and writing compare from this year to last year for the whole school, for specific grade levels, and for cohorts of students?

After you have determined what evidence you want to see and how you will secure that evidence, provide feedback, make adjustments, and designate someone to monitor the process. It could be someone in your school or, better yet, an outside consultant employed specifically to take on this task. The advantage of using an outside consultant, someone who regularly performs this kind of program-effectiveness evaluation, is that it provides a degree of objectivity that is ultimately in the best interest of full implementation of literacy learning.

Identify roles and responsibilities for literacy

Now that your action plan for a fail-safe system of literacy is complete, you'll want to think strategically about how to communicate it to your staff, students, school community, and district office. All these stakeholders must buy in to the plan and be willing to take on specific roles appropriate for their positions. Hopefully, you have been communicating the process all along so that the final communication is more of a formality— a time when you will ask for their commitment to your students becoming joyful, independent readers and writers.

Continuing to build capacity for growth in literacy behaviors will happen because you have a well-thought-out, data-driven plan to which your school community is committed. With the plan launched, you and your Literacy Leadership Team should consider all of the players and what their roles will be. Here are some thoughts to get you started.

The principal. The first and most important role for consideration is yours: the principal's. You are the vision keeper, the leader of leaders, the principal teacher in the school. As we know, you must model literacy behaviors. Everyone will take his or her cue from you—what you say, how you spend your time, and how you allocate resources. Think carefully about what role you can commit to and then be consistent. Part of that role will be hiring new staff members. Make it a priority to find and hire teachers who share your school's commitment to literacy and belief that all students can become joyful, independent readers and writers. If candidates have experience and training in the literacy behaviors that you have identified as components of the ideal literacy-focused classroom, so much the better.

> **Rose:** *When searching for three teachers to pilot a middle school literacy intervention, the principals in my district had difficulty finding volunteers within their schools. One principal was able to convince a special education teacher to take the position, but the other two principals found no one. I convinced a former secondary language arts and reading specialist to come out of retirement to teach in this exciting venture and found another new teacher so committed to students that she was willing to try anything! All three new hires led their students to exceptional gains in reading and writing. Based on this experience, I am convinced that the most important criteria in selecting teachers to improve reading and writing are 1) their belief that all students can learn to read and write, 2) their belief that they can successfully teach all students to read and write, and 3) their willingness to participate in professional development and consistently implement literacy behaviors on a daily basis.*

In the example just mentioned, when we eventually expanded the literacy intervention to many classrooms, we were surprised to discover that prior experience teaching literacy in a manner that contrasted with our expectations was often a hindrance. *Attitude* about the students, themselves, and *consistency* with literacy behaviors in the classroom had the most direct relationship to annual gains in reading and writing.

Finally, our conversations with principals who have documented measurable gains on the Florida Comprehensive Assessment Test over several years have turned out very consistent data about specific, literacy-focused action: These principals make selecting personnel for improving reading and writing a priority. They invest in new learning tools to meet the needs of all learners. Finally, they invest in professional development for themselves and their entire staff.

The school's leadership team. Each person in your school's leadership team should have a designated role. Does your school have one administrator responsible for each grade level? Certain administrators assigned to certain departments? In either case, each administrator's role might be to monitor, observe, give feedback, and make recommendations for the teachers within his or her area of responsibility. If you have one administrator responsible for the budget, this person might monitor textbook orders and other spending decisions. Another administrator might be responsible for overseeing professional development, in which case he or she must be articulate and conversant in the essential understandings of the literacy outcomes you are working toward.

The literacy resource teacher. After the principal, no one is more important than the in-school literacy resource teacher, dedicated to improving student achievement through gains in reading and writing. We recommend investing heavily in this person's professional development so that he or she becomes a literacy expert, relieved of regular classroom responsibilities and devoted full time to your literacy efforts. In this capacity, the literacy resource teacher's role is to provide ongoing professional development for the teaching staff, bring professional development opportunities to your (or the appropriate administrator's) attention, disseminate recent research, and serve as the number one collegial coach. If you don't have such a position in your school, we highly recommend that you budget for this support as soon as possible.

Reading, language arts, and English teachers. This group of teachers is responsible for producing continued measurable growth in students' reading and writing. The main obstacle at the middle school and high school levels is that many teachers believe students should already be reading and writing on grade level and if they are not, it's someone else's problem. As the literacy leader, your role is to help reading, language arts, and English teachers to embrace the daily consistent practice of literacy behaviors to help all students become proficient, joyful readers and writers Their role is to accept that challenge and to take this responsibility seriously. The rest of the faculty will watch to see how these teachers teach. If they don't incorporate literacy behaviors into their instruction, the content teachers most assuredly will not.

Content teachers. At the middle and high school levels, teachers of science, social studies, mathematics, world languages, art, music, technology, or any other class that's not reading, language arts, or English, are most appropriately focused on ensuring that their students exceed the set content standards. Within a fail-safe literacy system, their role is to model the literacy behaviors set out in Section 4 of your action plan. Through professional development, they will learn that by incorporating literacy processes, before, during, and after reading comprehension strategies, and accountable independent reading in content area nonfiction, their students will learn content faster, understand it at a deeper level, and remember it longer.

The Literacy Leadership Team. This group is very important for ongoing capacity building and schoolwide support for literacy learning. We believe the more that members of this team learn about reading and writing, the more responsibility they will want to take on. Representation from each grade, department, gender group, age group, and ethnic group will help the team function in the best interest of all students. You may want to include a parent, student, or business partner to represent and be a liaison with others. You also might consider including a district administrator who will advocate for your school's needs. If you have a college or university with expertise in literacy, then a representative from that constituency can support your team with access to professional development, grants, and other benefits that come from partnering with higher education.

One of the important contributions the Literacy Leadership Team can make is to design support pieces for teachers and administrators, like those shown in Figures 6.2 (see page 112) and 6.3 (see page 114). Such support pieces can provide ongoing direction for self-monitoring, professional growth, and goal setting to round out the fail-safe system of literacy.

The media specialist/librarian. In any school, the media center or library communicates that school's philosophy toward reading and writing. Is your school's media center a place where the love of literacy is modeled and where all students are welcome to read, write, and explore learning tools? Or is it a quiet place where good readers go to check out books?

The staff members who manage the media center and select print and technological learning tools for the center set its tone and are in a position to greatly support literacy improvement throughout the school. For this reason, the media specialist should be on any advisory or decision-making teams regarding learning tools, literacy events, and professional development. Expenditures of funds that support the media center should be carefully targeted to support the action plan for a fail-safe system of literacy. As someone who loves reading and writing and is committed to learning for all students, the media specialist should be a key person in supporting book donation drives, celebrity readers, reading buddies, or special events.

Parents and parent groups. Individual parents and parent groups should also have defined roles. Parent support groups, advisory councils, and parent-teacher associations can support the quest for literacy through targeted fund-raisers, volunteer hours, tutoring hours, and the development of special events that support and celebrate reading and writing.

Involving individual parents and other family members in the literacy learning of middle and high school students shows that your school values families and their cultures as important sources of literacy and content learning. Rather than asking parents to "support reading and writing," which they certainly do, you might develop specific parental roles related to academic units and plans. There are lots of possibilities to explore. Perhaps every instructional unit could include assignments that parents and students could work on together, such as reading aloud, or exploring relevant Internet sites. Once the expectation to involve parents as partners in developing students' reading, writing, listening, speaking, viewing, and thinking is clear, teachers will think of many ways to do so. Provided that the school communicates its purposes and procedures well, the parents will respond. In our experience, parents of older students particularly appreciate substantive involvement in their child's progress, since opportunities to do so typically drop off dramatically after the elementary years.

The district office. It's pretty much a given that your district office will support school-based efforts to improve reading and writing. As previously suggested, you might take it a step further by including an influential and key person from the district office on your Literacy Leadership

Team. Through this involvement, you will ensure that the district has a deep understanding of your fail-safe system of literacy, rather than a superficial one. With this personal connection, you increase the odds that your program will receive more support, gain access to more resources, and possibly receive assistance with evaluation. Only confident school-level leadership will take this suggestion to include district leadership seriously, but with the fail-safe system in place, total confidence in results will be natural.

To promote accountability, we encourage you to include these role descriptions, along with any others you need to implement your fail-safe system of literacy, in your action plan, in your school's professional handbook, and in official job descriptions. Do not be surprised if some of the stakeholders are not comfortable with this level of specificity. Some may even choose to transfer to another school. Remember: Each vacant position presents you with another opportunity to hire someone who will move the school closer to your goal. With planning detailed to specific responsibilities, you will find that growth toward all students becoming joyful, independent readers and writers will move quickly.

Celebrate successes!

You and your school community—teachers, staff, parents, and students—have worked hard to implement a consistent philosophy and belief regarding reading and writing. You deserve to celebrate. We believe that regular individual, group, and schoolwide celebrations are absolutely essential to continued enthusiasm and continuous improvement.

Ideas for celebration are varied, and your staff will want input into the plan. You may want to recognize those teachers who complete professional development. You may want to replace a regular faculty meeting or two with sharing sessions focused on literacy strategies that work. You may decide to feature students or teachers sharing their favorite poem or book over your televised or audio announcements. You'll definitely want to take lots of pictures to document and display student and teacher progress throughout the school. Involve parents and community members in your celebrations by encouraging them to donate books to the media center in honor of loved ones. Community members can also be honored as celebrity readers and writers. Make this an honor featured in announcements.

All in all, you should have a plan for recognizing the successes of students, parents and community members, and faculty and staff. Be sure this plan has both short-term and long-term impact, ranging from impromptu recognitions to assemblies celebrating improvement in standardized test scores.

In the Classroom

It's a Friday morning, and I, a middle school principal, have a few minutes in my office . . . alone. It's just enough time to think about the incredible highs and the occasional lows we've experienced during this first year of our fail-safe system of literacy. On many occasions, while working to motivate the teachers and students around me, I found myself motivated as well. One thing is sure: I always found new energy in classroom visits spent watching teachers use picture books to open a content unit—reading aloud to engage student interest and build vocabulary. It was there that I saw students connecting with text—willingly reading, writing, and talking about what they were learning because they were finding personal meaning through the use of strategies.

Our school has lots of evidence demonstrating we're on the right track. Just at this moment in thought, I'm interrupted by a knock on my open door—eager students sent to escort me, the principal, to a classroom literacy celebration. I open the door wider to reveal two 6th graders beaming from ear to ear. "Good morning, ladies," I beam back. Their response is full of giggles, and they take me by the arm and lead me to the media center.

We enter the media center, and I notice that today it looks different. There are special stations set up to showcase student accomplishments. A large paper tree stretching from floor to ceiling hovers in one corner, with a painted island scene all around it; it represents *Island of the Blue Dolphins* by Scott O'Dell. Students there are perched on "rocks" (really cushions), reading and quietly listening to music. Student stories written and illustrated to respond to the book and to extend learning about the Pacific are displayed in an Author's Corner. Guests can ask for signed copies or read and comment in the comment section at the end of each story.

Other students are standing by displays they created—visual representations and narrative descriptions of what they have been reading and learning. There are advertisements for their favorite independent reading novels, complete with rich descriptions and artwork. One student wonders if we might contact the novels' publishers to see if they would be interested in these ads. A teacher and I suggest that perhaps we should showcase them on our school Web page instead, so that other students can get ideas for reading. It's clear to everyone who speaks with these students and sees their products that they have worked hard on reading, writing, and speaking in a reflective way about their learning.

The students can barely contain themselves. There is a new sense of self-confidence as they read, answer questions, and share experiences from their literacy-focused classrooms. Yes, they have advanced significantly in self-confidence; they also read better, write better, and have better oral communication regarding their content standards. I note the team of teachers who stand at various points of the room, beaming with pride and encouraging the students. I am pleased to see our administrators and other teachers have come by to lend support.

Parents who can do so have taken off work for an hour to join their children for this special celebration. I also see community leaders and partners in education mingling with students showcasing what they have learned. With the energy really building and the room buzzing with discussions and demonstrations, district leaders arrive. I can see from their faces that they are pleasantly surprised—after all, they never really expected this to happen in such an urban center! But it has, and we are celebrating and planning for its continuous improvement.

I manage to leave my escorts briefly to address the group and share my genuine pride in their hard work over the past year. I intentionally make my remarks brief because I want it to be clear who the *real* heroes are. One is LaShun, who comes to the microphone and, with a little nervousness, begins to share how last year she didn't like to read and nobody was going to make her! She had had no success in reading and wasn't about to look stupid in front of her friends. But this year, LaShun says, something happened to change her mind. "It was different in Ms. Williams's class," she explains. Ms. Williams hadn't given up on her. "In Ms. Williams's class, we got to use the computer, graphic organizers, learn about words without just always looking them up in the dictionary." LaShun pauses to catch her breath, then continues: "I know I can do anything now." Looking towards Ms. Williams, LaShun says, "I can read . . . that's why I know I can do anything."

Of course, it's hard to find a dry eye in the place! I am thinking to myself that this is one of the best celebrations I have ever experienced in my 15 years as an educator. Looking around, I see that through this celebration, we—faculty, parents, district and community leaders, and I—are renewing our commitment to believe and do all that we can so that all our students can make LaShun's testimony—so that they will become joyful, independent readers and writers. As we do so, we are recommitting ourselves to continue the hard work of our fail-safe system of literacy.

The program ends, and soon I am back in my office, reflecting on what has happened during the first year of our fail-safe system of literacy. Not only have students improved, but teachers, assistant principals, resource teachers, media specialists, community members, and parents have joined in our commitment to literacy learning and are acting on their roles! With this capacity building in place, I am confident that the upward spiral will continue next year . . . and in the years to come.

Review and reflection

Fail-safe literacy leadership is a never-ending cycle of learning and improvement. Once a celebration is concluded and the school is quiet again, reflect on what went well and what you want to modify, and then start the fail-safe literacy process all over again! It will go much faster now, as the faculty and Literacy Leadership Team understand the process, but it will still require hard work, as both groups will have definite ideas about needed actions. This time, teachers at other schools will have heard of your fail-safe system of literacy. Expect to receive calls and resumes from professionals interested in joining your school's team. And of course, you'll find another group of students anxious to begin their literacy learning in your school and on their way to becoming joyful, independent readers and writers!

Further reading in capacity building

Barth, R. (1990). *Improving schools from within*. San Francisco, CA: Jossey-Bass.

Lambert, L. (1998). *Building leadership capacity in schools*. Alexandria, VA: Association for Supervision and Curriculum Development.

Bibliography

Allen, J. (1995). *It's never too late: Leading adolescents to lifelong literacy.* Portsmouth, NH: Heinemann.

Allen, J. (1999). *Words, words, words: Teaching vocabulary in grades 4–12.* York, ME: Stenhouse Publishers.

Allen, J. (2000). *Yellow brick roads: Shared and guided paths to independent reading 4–12.* Portland, ME: Stenhouse Publishers.

Allen, J., & Gonzalez, K. (1998). *There's room for me here: Literacy workshop in the middle school.* York, ME: Stenhouse Publishers.

Allington, R. L. (Ed.). (1998). *Teaching struggling readers.* Newark, DE: International Reading Association.

Allington, R., & Cunningham, P. (1996). *Schools that work: Where all children read and write.* Boston: Addison-Wesley Educational Publishers, Inc.

Anderson, R. C., Wilson, P. T., & Fielding, L. C. (1988, Summer). Growth in reading and how children spend their time outside of school. *Reading Research Quarterly,* 28(3), 285–303.

Atwell, N. (1998). *In the middle: New understandings about writing, reading, and learning* (2nd ed.). Portsmouth, NH: Boynton/Cook.

Barth, R. (1990). *Improving schools from within.* San Francisco, CA: Jossey-Bass.

Beamon, G. W. (2001). *Teaching with adolescent learning in mind.* Arlington Heights, IL: SkyLight Professional Development.

Beers, K., & Samuels, B. G. (1998). *Into focus: Understanding and creating middle school readers.* Norwood, MA: Christopher-Gordon Publishers.

Billmeyer, R., & Barton, M. L. (1998). *Teaching reading in the content areas: If not me, then who?* Aurora, CO: McREL.

Blase, J., & Blase, J. (1998). *Handbook of instructional leadership: How really good principals promote teaching and learning.* Thousand Oaks, CA: Corwin.

Blase, J., & Blase, J. (2001). *Empowering teachers: What successful principals do.* Thousand Oaks, CA: Corwin.

Blasewitz, M., & Taylor, R. (1999, January). Attacking literacy with technology in an urban setting. *Middle School Journal, 30*(3), 33–39.

Brown, J. L., & Moffett, C. A. (1999). *The hero's journey: How educators can transform schools and improve learning.* Alexandria, VA: Association for Supervision and Curriculum Development.

Brown, J. E., & Stephens, E. C. (1995). *Teaching young adult literature: Sharing the connection.* Belmont, CA: Wadsworth Publishing.

Brozo, W. G., & Simpson, M. L. (1999). *Readers, teachers, learners: Expanding literacy across the content areas* (3rd ed.). Upper Saddle River, NJ: Merrill.

Buehl, D. (2001). *Classroom strategies for interactive learning* (2nd ed.). Newark, DE: International Reading Association.

Calkins, L. M. (1994). *The art of teaching writing.* Portsmouth, NH: Heinemann.

Carr, J. F., & Harris, D. E. (2001). *Succeeding with standards: Linking curriculum, assessment, and action planning.* Alexandria, VA: Association for Supervision and Curriculum Development.

Cognition and Technology Group at Vanderbilt University. (1994). Multimedia environments for developing literacy in at-risk students. In B. Means (Ed.), *Technology and Education Reform,* (pp. 3–56). San Francisco: Jossey-Bass.

Daniels, H., Bizar, M., & Zemelman, S. (2001). *Rethinking high school: Best practice in teaching, learning, and leadership.* Portsmouth, NH: Heinemann.

Donohue, P. L., Voekl, K. E., Campbell, J. R., & Mazzeo, J. (1999, March). *NAEP reading report card for the nation and states: Executive summary.* Available: http://nces.ed.gov/nationalreportcard/pubs/mail1998/199500html.

Erickson, H. L. (1998). *Concept-based curriculum: Teaching beyond the facts.* Thousand Oaks, CA: Corwin Press.

Hargreaves, A. (Ed.). (1997). *Rethinking educational change with heart and mind: 1997 ASCD yearbook.* Alexandria, VA: Association for Supervision and Curriculum Development.

Harris, D. E., & Carr, J. F. (1996). *How to use standards in the classroom.* Alexandria, VA: Association for Supervision and Curriculum Development.

Harvey, S. (1998). *Nonfiction matters: Reading, writing and research in grades 3–8.* York, ME: Stenhouse Publishers.

Harvey, S., & Goudvis, A. (2000). *Strategies that work: Teaching comprehension to enhance understanding.* York, ME: Stenhouse Publishers.

Hasselbring, T. S., Goin, L., Taylor, R., Bottge, B., & Daley, P. (1997, November). The computer doesn't embarrass me. *Educational Leadership, 55*(3), 30–33.

International Reading Association. (2001). *Supporting young adolescents' literacy learning: A joint position paper of the International Reading Association and National Middle School Association.* Newark, DE: Author. Available: http://www.reading.org/positions/supporting_young_adolesc.html.

Jensen, E. (1998). *Teaching with the brain in mind.* Alexandria, VA: Association for Supervision and Curriculum Development.

Joyce, B. (1990). *Changing school culture through staff development.* Alexandria, VA: Association for Supervision and Curriculum Development.

Joyce, B., & Showers, B. (2002). *Student achievement through staff development* (3rd ed.). Alexandria, VA: Association for Supervision and Curriculum Development.

Keene, E. O., & Zimmermann, S. (1997). *Mosaic of thought: Teaching comprehension in a reader's workshop.* Portsmouth, NH: Heinemann.

Lambert, L. (1998). *Building leadership capacity in schools.* Alexandria, VA: Association for Supervision and Curriculum Development.

Langer, J. A. (2000). *Achieving high quality reading and writing in an urban middle school: The case of Gail Slatko.* The National Center for English Language Learning & Achievement. Available: http://cela.albany.edu.

Little, J. W. (1993, Summer). Teachers' professional development in a climate of educational reform. *Educational Evaluational Policy Analysis, 15*(2), 129–152.

Marsh, D. D. (Ed.). (1999). *Preparing our schools for the 21st century: 1999 ASCD yearbook.* Alexandria, VA: Association for Supervision and Curriculum Development.

Marzano, R. J., Pickering, D. J., & Pollock, J. E. (2001). *Classroom instruction that works: Research-based strategies for increasing student achievement.* Alexandria, VA: Association for Supervision and Curriculum Development.

Murphy, J. (2001, October 9). *Leadership for literacy: Policy leverage points.* Paper presented at the Conference on Leadership for Literacy. Washington, DC: Educational Testing Service/Educational Commission of the States.

National Reading Panel. (2000). Teaching children to read: An evidence-based assessment of the scientific research literature on reading and its implications for reading instruction. Washington, DC: U.S. Department of Health and Human Services.

Patton, S., & Holmes, M. (Eds.). (1998). *The keys to literacy.* Washington, DC: Council for Basic Education.

Robb, L. (2000). *Teaching reading in middle school.* New York: Scholastic Professional Books.

Romano, T. (1995). *Writing with passion: Life stories, multiple genres.* Portsmouth, NH: Boynton/Cook.

Routman, R. (1994). *Invitations: Changing teachers and learners K–12* (2nd ed.). Portsmouth, NH: Heinemann.

Sergiovanni, T. J. (1996). *Leadership for the schoolhouse: How is it different? Why is it important?* San Francisco: Jossey-Bass Publishers.

Sergiovanni, T. J. (2000). *The lifeworld of leadership: Creating culture, community, and personal meaning in our schools.* San Francisco: Jossey-Bass Publishers.

Sergiovanni, T. J. (2001). *The principalship: A reflective practice perspective* (4th ed.). Needham Heights, MA: Pearson Education.

Schmoker, M. (1999). *Results: The key to continuous school improvement* (2nd ed.). Alexandria, VA: Association for Supervision and Curriculum Development.

Schmoker, M. (2001). *The results fieldbook: Practical strategies from dramatically improved schools.* Alexandria, VA: Association for Supervision and Curriculum Development.

Smith, W. F., & Andrews, R. L. (1989). *Instructional leadership: How principals make a difference.* Alexandria, VA: Association for Supervision and Curriculum Development.

Snow, C., Burns, M. S., & Griffin, P. (1998). *Preventing reading difficulties in young children*. Washington, DC: National Academy Press.

Sprenger, M. (1999). *Learning and memory: The brain in action*. Alexandria, VA: Association for Supervision and Curriculum Development.

Stephens, E. C., & Brown, J. E. (2000). *A handbook of content literacy strategies: 75 practical reading and writing ideas*. Norwood, MA: Christopher-Gordon Publishers.

Taylor, R. (1999, December). Missing pieces: Aligned curriculum, instruction, and assessment. *Schools in the Middle, 9*(4), 14–16.

Taylor, R. (2001, October). Steps to literacy. *Principal Leadership, 2*(2) 34–39.

Taylor, R. (2001, Fall). Teacher's challenge. *Journal of Staff Development, 22*(4), 56–59.

Taylor, R. (2002, September). Creating a system that gets results for older, reluctant readers. *Phi Delta Kappan, 84*(1) 85–87.

Taylor, R., Hasselbring, T. S., & Williams, R. D. (2001, October). Reading, writing, and misbehavior. *Principal Leadership, 2*(2), 34–39.

Tovani, C. (2000). *I read it, but I don't get it: Comprehension strategies for adolescent readers*. Portland, ME: Stenhouse Publishers.

Weaver, C. (Ed.). (1998). *Lessons to share on teaching grammar in context*. Portsmouth, NH: Boynton/Cook.

Wiggins, G., & McTighe, J. (1998). *Understanding by design*. Alexandria, VA: Association for Supervision and Curriculum Development.

Wilhelm, J. D. (2001). *Strategic reading guiding students to lifelong literacy grades 6–12*. Portsmouth, NH: Boynton/Cook.

Wilson, E. (1999). *Reading at the middle and high school levels: Building active readers across the curriculum*. Arlington, VA: Educational Research Service.

Wolfe, P. (2001). *Brain matters: Translating research into classroom practice*. Alexandria, VA: Association for Supervision and Curriculum Development.

Index

About the Authors

Rosemarye (Rose) Taylor (primary author) is an assistant professor of Educational Leadership at the University of Central Florida, specializing in instructional leadership with an emphasis on literacy. She has a rich literacy background that includes experience as a middle and high school reading, language arts, and Spanish teacher. She has also served as a high school assistant principal and a middle school principal and has been a district administrator in both urban and small city systems.

In addition to her current academic responsibilities, Rose works in the private sector developing and delivering literacy-focused professional development for teachers and administrators. She serves as consultant on literacy, learning communities, curriculum, and leadership to schools, districts, and professional organizations like Phi Delta Kappa and on middle school reform (focused on literacy) with The Galef Institute. Her articles have appeared in numerous journals, including *Educational Leadership, Kappan, Middle School Journal, Schools in the Middle, American Secondary Education, AASA Professor, The National Staff Development Journal, Principal Leadership, Kappa Delta Pi Record,* and *The School Administrator.*

From 1993–1999, Rose led the research, design, and implementation of the Orange County (Fla.) Literacy Program, which has positively affected thousands of elementary, middle, and high school students and teachers, and is now the foundation for Scholastic Inc.'s intervention and literacy programs for middle and high school students. The classroom concept designed under Rose's leadership has been produced as a product by Scholastic Inc. (including software from Vanderbilt) and implemented internationally.

You may contact Rose at 3813 Blazing Star Drive, Orlando, Florida 32828, or via e-mail at rtaylor@mail.ucf.edu.

Valerie Doyle Collins (secondary author) is president of VL Collins Consulting, Inc., an organization focused on promoting and advancing literacy and literacy leadership. As a literacy consultant, she works with school districts throughout the United States and abroad. She spends much of her time providing professional development services while serving as a coach, mentor, and change catalyst for districts and schools targeting literacy learning for all students, especially the older struggling reader. Valerie is also a contributing author and consultant for the Literacy First Process, a comprehensive, research-based reading reform process designed for pre-K–12.

Valerie has spent the majority of her career working with school populations that have a high percentage of reluctant readers. Her experience first as a high school assistant principal and then as the principal of an urban middle school focused on literacy has provided her with valuable insight to motivate educators and provide support and training needed to ensure classroom success with middle and high school students.

You may contact Valerie at 1208 Deer Lake Circle, Apopka, Florida 32712, or at www.vlcollins.com.

Related ASCD Resources: Developing Literacy

Audiotapes

Literacy and Standards: Across the Content by Robin Fogarty (#202290)
Literacy and Learning in the Multi-Age Classroom by Barbara Michelutti (#200203)
Teaching and Assessing Reading in the Content Area by Rachel Billmeyer (#297243)

CD-ROM and Multimedia

Reading Strategies for the Content Areas: An ASCD Action Tool (#703109)

Print Products

50 Literacy Strategies: Step by Step by Gail E. Tompkins (#301307)
Essential Ingredients: Recipes for Teaching Writing by Sandra Worsham (#101241)
Teaching Reading in the Content Areas: If Not Me, Then Who? (2nd ed.) by Rachel Billmeyer and Mary Lee Barton (#397258)
Teaching Reading in Mathematics (2nd ed.) by Mary Lee Barton and Clare Heidema (#302053)
Teaching Reading in Science by Mary Lee Barton and Deborah L. Jordan (#302269)

Videotapes

Implementing a Reading Program in Secondary Schools (tape and facilitator's guide) (#402033)
The Lesson Collection: Reading Strategies 2 (8-tape series) (#402034)
Reading in the Content Areas Video Series (3-tape series and online facilitator's guide) (#402029)

For additional information, visit us on the World Wide Web (http://www.ascd.org), send an e-mail message to member@ascd.org, call the ASCD Service Center (1-800-933-ASCD or 703-578-9600, then press 2), send a fax to 703-575-5400, or write to Information Services, ASCD, 1703 N. Beauregard St., Alexandria, VA 22311-1714 USA.